Kris Dhillon

The New
Curry Secret

KRIS DHILLON

THE NEW CURRY SECRET

FIREFLY BOOKS

A Firefly Book

Published by Firefly Books Ltd. 2009

Published by Right Way, an imprint of Constable & Robinson, 2009

First printing

Publisher Cataloging-in-Publication Data (U.S.)

Dhillon, Kris.
   The new curry secret : mouthwatering Indian restaurant dishes
to cook at home / Kris Dhillon.
[192] p. : col. photos. ; cm.
Includes index.
ISBN-13: 978-1-55407-561-4 (pbk.)
ISBN-10: 1-55407-561-0 (pbk.)
1. Cookery (Curry). I. Title.
641.6384 dc22 TX819.C9D555   2009

Published in the United States by
Firefly Books (U.S.) Inc.
P.O. Box 1338, Ellicott Station
Buffalo, New York 14205

Library and Archives Canada Cataloguing in Publication

Dhillon, Kris
   The new curry secret : mouthwatering Indian restaurant
dishes to cook with at home / Kris Dhillon.

Includes index.
ISBN-13: 978-1-55407-561-4
ISBN-10: 1-55407-561-0
   1. Indian Cookery. 2. Cookery (Curry). I. Title.
TX724.5.I4D45 2009   641.5954   C2009-902651-1

Published in Canada by
Firefly Books Ltd.
66 Leek Crescent
Richmond Hill, Ontario L4B 1H1

Designed and produced by Basement Press, London
www.basementpress.com
Photography by Nicholas Christopher

Picture credits: p.17: creative commons — Henrique Vicente;
p.19: creative commons — thebittenworld.com; p.23: creative commons — Judepics.

Printed and bound in China

THIS BOOK is dedicated to all the curry fans who helped make the original *The Curry Secret* such a huge success. It gives me great pleasure to know that the book inspired so many to follow their passion and enthusiasm for Indian restaurant curries. Well, now in turn, their vigor and enthusiasm have inspired me to write this book, *The New Curry Secret*, especially for them. It is for curry lovers like them that I have put together a selection of sensational new recipes and revealed even more, to help take their curry cooking to a new level. Never again will phrases like "chef's special spice blend" or "chef's secret recipe" on an Indian restaurant menu baffle and perplex anyone. The secrets are all in here.

Happy curry cooking.

Kris Dhillon
www.krisdhillon.com

Contents

1.   INTRODUCTION

INDIA IS A land of stark contrasts and startling paradoxes, and a culture with the kind of complexity, mystique and intrigue that develops only with a long, eventful and, at times, colorful history.

Many historians believe that Indian history and its cuisine are as old as humankind itself, evolving over the ages under the influences of travelers and invaders from all corners of the world, and from the emergence of various religions, rulers and cultures internally.

Despite this, Indian cuisine has not lost its original identity. It has instead become richer and more diverse, while managing to retain the core principle that everything we eat should be pure and balanced. Onions, garlic, ginger and spices, integral to Indian cuisine, have proven health-giving properties. Cook your curries with healthy oils such as olive, sunflower and safflower, using ghee, butter and cream in moderation, and you will have a diet that is not only compatible with a healthy lifestyle but one that contributes to it.

Indian cuisine is wonderfully rich and varied. The regional variations reflect the historical influences, contrasting demographics, culture and ethnicity of this vast and exotic subcontinent. With a multitude of vibrant dishes flavored with aromatic spice blends (*masalas)* and fresh fragrant herbs, it is not hard to understand why Indian food has become a firm favorite all over the Western world.

Traditional Indian cuisine is split into four categories: north Indian, south Indian, east Indian and west Indian. However, ask for a chicken tikka masala anywhere in India, and it is likely that all you will get is a blank look. Going out for curry is not an Indian pastime, but in the West, and Britain in particular, it is a ritual that many people relish with gusto. Chicken tikka masala is reportedly the most frequently consumed dish in Britain and is even more popular than fish and chips.

The cuisine of Indian restaurants, loved by millions, does not fit into any of the traditional Indian cuisine categories, but it embraces some aspect of each, becoming in itself quite unique. It is this cuisine that holds the uncompromising, tantalizing allure for the vast majority of curry lovers in the West. The traditional recipes, as wonderful as they are, simply don't "have it" when your tastebuds are crying out for the distinct, deep "curryish" flavor and aroma of restaurant curries.

Indian restaurant cuisine has its origins in the period of the British Raj. Indian cooks, pressed by their British masters to prepare meals that were more acceptable to the British palate, produced modified traditional dishes for which the British rapidly acquired a taste. So much so, that the first Indian restaurants were opened in the affluent parts of London so that British officers returning home from their duties in India were not deprived of their favorite foods. This was the beginning of a new cuisine.

The second phase in the evolution of this new cuisine took place in the mid-1900s as families from Bangladesh, migrating to England to make their fortune, opened Indian restaurants in the East End of London, an area still famous for this cuisine.

A number of anglicized Indian dishes were created during that early period, including the well-known and loved chicken tikka masala. Later in the century there was a rapid proliferation of balti houses serving delicately spiced curries, freshly cooked in a woklike pan. Beginning in Birmingham this new phenomenon rapidly spread to other parts of the country. The balti dishes served in Indian restaurants are descendants of this cooking style and remain popular to this day.

In fact, Indian restaurant food has continued to grow in popularity all over the world. The United States' Immigration Act of 1965 saw an influx of Asian immigration to the U.S. and with it a surge of Indian restaurants, especially in San Francisco, Los Angeles, Houston, Chicago and New York. All-you-can-eat buffets with an array of standard dishes are common in many Indian restaurants in the United States, catering for a growing appetite for Indian food among the locals.

Indian restaurants are also common throughout Canada, particularly in Toronto and Vancouver where large numbers of Indian nationals have settled since 1970. The cuisine of South Africa also boasts several dishes of Indian origin; some have evolved over time to become unique to South Africa while many others are recognizably traditional Indian preparations modified with local spices.

In Australia the popularity of Indian food has increased considerably in the last 20 years, resulting in a rapid growth in the availability of Indian food and ingredients. Nearly all Australian towns and cities now enjoy the existence of several good Indian restaurants and eateries, and more are opening each month.

There has emerged an avid and enthusiastic demand for dishes that challenge the modern Western palate, rather than pander to the tastes of yesteryear when recipes were adapted to create milder dishes like chicken korma and chicken tikka masala that were gentler on the tastebuds. Indian food is now integral to the Western diet and restaurateurs have responded by creating more authentic dishes with a "no-holds barred" approach to the use of more pungent spices and herbs.

There has also been a period of culinary evolution around the globe with a growing homogenization or mixing of cooking styles and techniques. Worldwide, professional chefs have sought to develop and promote the intermingling of a variety of popular cuisines, resulting in what has become widely known as "fusion" food. Indian chefs too have embraced these developments and Indian spring rolls, dhal soup and *murgh* (chicken) Ceylon are now commonplace on the Indian restaurant menu. While the favorites of the past decades remain popular, these elements of change have seen many more inventive restaurateurs create new and vibrant dishes.

In this book I seek to provide curry lovers with the know-how for creating these new and exquisite restaurant dishes. *The New Curry Secret* will show you how you can create the delicious restaurant curries of today, simply and easily. I have included all the closely held secrets, the special spice blends and tricks of the trade employed by Indian chefs, plus some labor-saving tips and ideas to make it even easier when cooking Indian restaurant food at home.

The New Curry Secret will help you take your cooking to the next level. Not only does it give you a plethora of delicious recipes and cooking ideas, it goes a step further. It shows you what makes a good cook great; how you can transform good dishes into mouthwatering delights that are a feast for the senses just by using a few simple techniques.

In this book you will discover the closely guarded secrets of Indian chefs. You will be surprised, delighted and amazed to learn how you too can easily produce delicious restaurant curries at home; curries that are as good, if not better, than the ones you enjoy in your favorite Indian restaurant.

THE "NO SMELL" CURRY SAUCE

It is the curry sauce that, more than anything else, influences the flavor, appearance and texture of the typical restaurant curry and differentiates it from the traditional homemade one. It is also the curry sauce that enables you to cook one or more fabulous restaurant curries in next to no time. Have a quantity of this sauce on hand and you can put together an array of delicious, authentic restaurant curries in a matter of minutes.

However, there is no such thing as a free lunch — the smell of boiling onions drives everyone out of the house for hours! Well, not any more! The new curry sauce will have them staying right where they are; it actually smells good while it's cooking.

By making a few changes to the way the curry sauce is made, the unpleasant smell that emanated from the saucepan during the boiling stage has been eliminated. If you don't like the smell when making the curry sauce as outlined in other Indian cookbooks, you will love the new recipe.

Kris Dhillon

2. What makes a good cook great?

W HAT IS IT that makes a good cook great? What enables some cooks to take an ordinary, everyday dish and lift it to another dimension? The answer, as to most seemingly difficult questions, is a simple one — the best and the freshest ingredients available, and a passion for food. Many people believe that poor-quality meat and stale vegetables can be disguised by putting them in a curry. This is completely inaccurate. A good Indian dish is a balance of spicy flavors around fresh, tasty vegetables and good-quality meat or fish. No amount of sugar and spice can disguise tasteless, stale or out-of-season ingredients.

I'm not sure what kindled my own passion for food, but whatever it was, it saw me standing on a stool so that I could reach the stove at the tender age of 7 to make my first chapati — under the watchful eye of my mother, of course.

My family moved from India to England in the late 1950s when I was just 5, and food always played an important part in our lives. It was difficult to buy many of the exotic ingredients that are so readily available today, so my parents grew whatever they could in their garden. Meat was somewhat scarce and expensive in the years after the Second World War and, even though it was eaten only once or twice a week, it was common for those early migrants to buy cheaper, tougher cuts of meat and chicken, and they developed inventive and clever methods of cooking them.

With my emerging interest in food and cooking I loved to watch my father cook the weekly meat curry. He would throw pieces of mutton, cheaper cuts of pork or portions of chicken into a large aluminum pot together with a quantity of chopped onions and some salt. The pot was placed on a gentle heat and cooked slowly for up to three hours until the onions had melted and the meat was beautifully tender. He would then add generous amounts of ghee (clarified butter), ripe tomatoes, garlic, ginger, turmeric and freshly ground spices (which my mother had painstakingly ground to a fine powder with a pestle and mortar) until the colorless simmering mass was a fragrant, rich, golden red.

Just when you thought it couldn't get any better, in would go the spring onions plucked straight from the garden. Fresh green fenugreek leaves, again picked just before using, were roughly chopped and stirred in. Occasionally, if they were growing in the garden, my father would add sliced turnips or carrots or even spinach leaves, harvested at the last minute of course, and simmer them with the meat during the last hour or so of cooking. Finally, a generous sprinkling of freshly picked cilantro would complete the culinary exercise. The aromas made your mouth water.

The fresh, aromatic vibrancy of those last few ingredients added so much to the character, flavor and appearance of these dishes that they were transformed from being just good to being absolutely sublime.

My growing passion was further kindled when my mother decided to take me back to India for the first time since I had left the country some 12 years earlier. Expecting to be bored with and alienated by a country I had little memory of and possibly little in common with, I instead landed in a place that so fascinated me I tingled with excitement. The land that my parents farmed before they left for England had been well looked after and traditionally (organically) farmed by our extended family. The fields were full of corn, sugarcane, spinach, mustard greens, chilies, radishes, turnips, carrots, squash, eggplants, spring onions, garlic and herbs and edible, exotic plants that I had never seen or heard of before. The people were different too: solid, pragmatic, salt-of-the-earth type individuals who were clearly in harmony with their environment and all its inhabitants.

Mealtimes were an absolute delight. My young cousins and I would rise early in the morning to make the short journey to the fields to pick the vegetables — eggplants, zucchini, tender green chickpeas, turnips or carrots, chilies — and herbs for making breakfast, the meal consisting of a vegetable bhaji or dhal, buttery parathas, yogurt that had been made overnight, homemade green mango or lime *achar* (pickle) and *lassi* (buttermilk — a light, fresh-tasting liquid that remains after yogurt is churned to make butter, done early each morning). Chai, flavored with cardamom, made with fresh buffalo milk obtained that morning and sweetened with rich, sweet, raw cane sugar (*jaggery*), followed shortly after.

When lunch- and dinnertime came around, the vegetables and herbs collected earlier were "stale." "Feed them to the cattle," my aunt would say, "and go pick some more." A few hours old, and they were no longer considered fresh enough for human consumption. Leftover yogurt from the day before was no longer eaten with meals as a side dish, but soured and thickened with chickpea flour (*besan*), flavored with green fenugreek, whole spices, cilantro and lots of fresh green chilies and made into a delicious curry. Any milk left over from the previous day was not fresh enough to drink and was either made into dessert using rice, sago or vermicelli, or curdled and made into *paneer* for cooking with ginger, garlic, tomatoes, chilies and peas to make mattar paneer. Vegetables were so fresh that you didn't need to add water to make a sauce; their juices were copious enough.

Yet there was still more to come; I was fortunate enough to be in India at the time of year that sugarcane is harvested and milled to squeeze out the juice. What a wonderful experience. I would eagerly arise at the chilly crack of dawn and make my way down to the mill, jug in hand. I had only a little memory of drinking freshly squeezed sugarcane juice

(*ras*) and what a heavenly delight it was when I tasted it again for the first time. The cool, fresh sweetness of it was extraordinary.

These experiences were a revelation to me of how good food should be, but there is one particular incident that somehow transcended all of this and crystallized for me the sheer essence of fresh food. I loved to walk barefoot through the cool channels of water as they irrigated the fields, taking in this pure, bountiful countryside that they call the Punjab. During one such excursion, I leaned over and pulled a carrot out of the ground, shook it around in the water to wash off the soil and bit into it. The depth of flavor, the freshness of the aroma, the sweet, juicy "carroty" taste were so pure and intense, it made me stop in my tracks and savor its stunning uniqueness. I had never tasted such true flavor before. It was as though my tastebuds came truly alive only at that moment. This experience made such an impression on me that I have recounted it many times. It was only a carrot, but I had never tasted anything like it, and the experience has shaped my relationship with food to this day.

The days were filled with delightful, mouthwatering episodes at every turn, beginning early with a long, cool, delicious glass of ras and ending quite late with fresh cobs of corn roasted in the embers of a dying fire followed by a glass of warm milk sweetened with raw cane sugar. I thought this must be paradise. I took great delight in learning to make new and complex dishes from my grandmother and aunts who were wonderful and creative cooks.

I became enthralled and enchanted by this mystical land, its people and the rich and sustainable lives they lived. They used no chemicals or foreign substances on the land. They looked after their animals, feeding them wholesome crops, linseeds and herbs. They used and reused everything. The remnants of harvested corn and milled sugarcane were fed to the cattle or used as compost. Cattle and buffalo manure was used on the land or made into patties, dried and used as fuel for cooking and heating. Even the ashes that remained after the patties were burned were used for scouring pots and pans. There was no packaging, no waste and no landfill. Practices the West thought of as primitive then are now, with our awareness of climate change, seen to be environmentally friendly and ecologically sound.

I reluctantly returned to England after several months, but the essence of this magical country lives inside me to this day.

TIPS ON BUYING AND USING FRESH INGREDIENTS

If you want to cook great Indian food, it is important that you obtain fresh, top-quality ingredients, preferably organically produced. Just as you cannot make a silk purse out of a sow's ear, you cannot create a culinary masterpiece from stale, tasteless produce.

■ Buy seasonal fruit and vegetables. It is possible nowadays to buy just about every type of fruit and vegetable at any time of year, but at what cost to your tastebuds and your wallet? Out-of-season fruit is generally tasteless and vegetables are bland and sometimes even bitter. Produce that is in season will taste a lot better and cost significantly less.

■ Buy local produce. Local markets and farmers' markets are good places to buy seasonal, fresh produce. You will be helping to save the planet too as the food has not traveled so far.

■ Buy the more exotic ingredients from Indian grocers. You will find the quality is top-notch and the prices are lower.

■ When buying fruit and vegetables, pick them up, examine them and smell them. If they are fresh, they should be plump with smooth skins, feel heavy for their size and have a distinct aroma. Bunches of herbs should not be tired and wilting.

■ Buy organically grown produce when you can or grow some of your own. The appearance, feel and scent of really fresh produce, especially fresh herbs, are truly wonderful.

A little goes a long way to adding that touch of magic to your dishes. Try some of the following:

■ Homegrown cilantro (also referred to as coriander), for example, is so much more vibrant and aromatic than anything you can buy. Just a little sprinkled on the dish transforms it into something special, and you can grow it in a tiny area of your garden or even in a pot. During the warmer months, just sprinkle some coriander seeds from your pantry onto the garden or onto some potting mix in a pot, sprinkle some soil or potting mix on top, water and keep moist. It's that easy. Fresh cilantro is a delicate herb. Use it toward the end of cooking and as a garnish.

■ Next time you have some garlic cloves or onions that are beginning to sprout, plant them in the garden. They will grow healthy green shoots in no time. Use the green tops, roughly chopped, next time you make a curry or savory snack, and you will add an extra dimension of flavor, color and aroma to the dish. Both of these ingredients need to be cooked so use them at the beginning of making a dish. (Note: much of the garlic available nowadays is imported and treated with a gas that effectively kills it, so it will not sprout. Buy organic garlic bulbs if you wish it to sprout and it will grow beautifully.)

■ Throw some fenugreek seeds (again the same fenugreek seeds you use for cooking) onto a small area in the garden or into a pot and within a couple of weeks you will have fresh, green fenugreek leaves. Add a handful, chopped, to curries, bhajis, pakoras or really just

about any savory dish to impart a robust flavor to the dish. Fresh fenugreek requires cooking, so use it at the beginning.

■ A few fresh mint leaves shredded and sprinkled onto a salad or stirred into yogurt or even a curry add liveliness, color and flavor. Mint grows easily and is a perennial. Ask a friend who has some growing in the garden to pull out a few roots, and put them into a pot or straight into your garden. You will have fresh mint from late spring to early winter every year.

■ If you have a handful of sweet, ripe cherry tomatoes, stir them whole or sliced in half into the dish at the last minute and you will introduce additional color, texture and taste. The appearance of the dish is beautifully enhanced. Remember you feast with your eyes before your mouth.

Throughout the book, I have included suggestions for the use of one or more optional ingredients such as those above, and given instructions on how best to use them in your cooking. Please remember, though, you can make perfectly good dishes by following the basic recipes; these suggestions are an optional extra for those times when you are in the mood to create something extraordinary.

3. What's in season?

THERE ARE many good reasons why we should eat food that is produced locally and in season:

- Locally sourced, in-season food is fresher, tastier, more nutritious and less expensive.
- Due to the fewer "food miles" that local produce travels, there is a lower consumption of energy and therefore less CO_2 emission.
- The more you buy locally, the more you support your local community.

Clearly not all fruit and vegetables can be grown in all climates, and when local produce is scarce it is better to source food from neighboring countries rather than those on the other side of the planet. The following list is a brief guide of what is best each season:

WINTER
Vegetables — Artichokes, beets, brussels sprouts, cauliflowers, kale, leeks, parsnips, potatoes, pumpkins, rhubarb, rutabaga, turnips, winter squash
Fruit — Apples, bananas, clementines, cranberries, kiwi fruit, lemons, oranges, blood oranges, pears, pineapples

SPRING
Vegetables — Asparagus, broccoli, carrots, cauliflowers, eggplant, leeks, new potatoes, radishes, spinach, spring greens, spring onions
Fruit — Apples, bananas, kiwi fruit, lemons, oranges, blood oranges, pomegranates

SUMMER
Vegetables — Broad beans, runner beans, carrots, chard, cucumbers, eggplant, fennel, garlic, okra, onions, peas, sweet peppers, potatoes, radishes, spring onions, summer squash, sweet corn, zucchini
Fruit — Apricots, blackberries, blueberries, cherries, gooseberries, grapes, kiwi fruit, mangoes, melons, peaches, raspberries, strawberries, tomatoes

AUTUMN
Vegetables — Broccoli, butternut squash, carrots, celery, chard, eggplant, garlic, wild mushrooms, onions, parsnips, sweet peppers, potatoes, rutabaga, summer squash, sweet corn, turnips, zucchini
Fruit — Apples, blackberries, clementines, figs, grapes, melons, nectarines, peaches, pears, pineapples, plums, quince

4.

EVERY region of India brings its own unique influence and subtle variations to the popular dishes you enjoy in your favorite Indian restaurants. Spices that are fragrant, pungent, sharp, spicy, earthy and warm, and expertly blended are the essence of Indian cuisine. It is said that the flavors are as varied as the climate of India and as exotic as the people.

HINDI/PUNJABI	ENGLISH	HINDI/PUNJABI	ENGLISH
achar	pickle — sour	gajar	carrot
adrak	ginger	garam masala	spice mix
aloo	potato	ghee	clarified butter
amb	mango	gobhi	cauliflower
balti*	karahi dish	haldi	turmeric
bengan/brinjal	eggplant	hari dal	green mung beans
bhaji	vegetable	hing	asafetida
bhindi	okra	imli	tamarind
chai	tea	jaggery/goor	raw cane sugar/molasses
chana	chickpeas	jaifal	nutmeg
chatani	chutney or pickle	jangli dalchini	cassia bark/chinese cinnamon
chawal	rice	jeera/zeera	cumin
dahi	yogurt	jinga	shrimp
dalchini	cinnamon	kali elaichi	black cardamom
dhal	pulses	kali mirch	pepper
dhanya	cilantro	kalonjii	onion seeds
dudh	milk	karahi	woklike pan or serving dish
elaichi	cardamom		
faal	fruit		

*In Hindi and Punjabi *balti* actually means "bucket." The word has taken on a new meaning within the context of the restaurant menu.

Hindi/Punjabi	English	Hindi/Punjabi	English
keema	minced meat	piaz	onions
kela	banana	pootna	mint
kesar	saffron	raai	mustard seed
kulfi	ice cream made with condensed milk	raita	spiced vegetable yogurt
		rajma	red kidney beans
kumbh/khumba	mushrooms	ras	juice
lasan	garlic	roti	chapati
lassi	yogurt drink	saag	pureed spinach and green leafy vegetables
lowng	cloves		
machli	fish	sabji	vegetables
maki	corn	sakara/kand	sugar
malai	cream	sarson/saron	mustard greens
marss	meat	saunf	fennel
masala	blend of spices	shev	apple
masoor	lentils	shorba	soup, gravy
mattar	peas	suwa	dill
methi	fenugreek	takrai	lemongrass
mirch	chilies, pepper	tamatar	tomato
murghi	chicken	tandoor	clay oven
namak/loorn	salt	tava	hot plate for cooking
nariyal	coconut	tej patta	bay leaf
nimbu	lemon	til	sesame seed
paani	water	tulsi	basil
palak	spinach	tur (toovar)	pigeon peas
paneer	cheese	zafrani	saffron

5. Getting started

S pices are integral to Indian food. They add warmth, pungency, heat and the distinct aroma and flavor of Indian dishes. Creative chefs may use a dozen or more spices in one dish, but most cooks will do fine with a quantity of garam masala and one or two additional ingredients. You may want to keep other spices handy for particular dishes.

Essential spices and herbs
Essential ingredients
- green cardamom pods
- black cardamom pods
- coriander seeds
- black peppercorns
- cinnamon
- cumin seeds
- cloves
- nutmeg
- bay leaves
- mustard seeds
- turmeric powder
- chili powder

You will require the first nine ingredients in the list above to make garam masala.

Other useful ingredients
- fennel seeds
- fenugreek seeds
- paprika
- onion seeds
- green mango powder (*ambchoor*)
- tamarind
- dried fenugreek leaves (*methi*)
- carom or ajowan seeds (*ajwain*)
- chat masala

Buying and storing spices

Spices are at their best when used within three months or so of purchase. Buy spices from an Indian grocer rather than a supermarket. Prices will be lower and the quality a lot better. To ensure maximum freshness and taste, buy whole spices rather than powders, and grind only in quantities that are likely to be used up within three or four weeks.

Store spices in glass, stainless steel or ceramic containers with tightly fitting lids, in a cool, dark and dry place.

HOW TO MAKE YOGURT

Bring 35 fl oz (2.1 US pints/1 L) of organic milk to a boil and cool until warm. Transfer the milk to a bowl or other container with a lid and stir in 2 tablespoons of live plain yogurt. Wrap the container in a tea towel and put in a warm place for 4–5 hours until set. Refrigerate.

HOW TO MAKE PANEER

Bring 70 fl oz (4.2 US pints/2 L) of organic milk to a boil, turn down the heat and stir in the juice of a lemon. Continue to stir until the milk solids separate from the whey — add a few drops of vinegar if it doesn't completely separate. Strain the milk through a colander lined with muslin. Allow to drain for a few minutes, then take up the muslin and squeeze out excess moisture. Gently shape the paneer still in the muslin so that it is about 1/2 inch (1.5 cm) thick. Place on a hard surface and put a large saucepan filled with water or other heavy object on top to help squeeze out all the moisture. Leave for an hour and cut the paneer into cubes.

HOW TO CLARIFY BUTTER TO MAKE GHEE

Gently heat 1 lb 2 oz (500 g) of organic butter in a small saucepan until completely melted. Continue to heat for 15–20 minutes until the solids sink to the bottom. Skim the surface, allow to cool a little, and strain the ghee into a suitable dish.

OTHER KEY INGREDIENTS

Every region has its favorite ingredients and Indian restaurant cuisine embraces and reflects the flavors and diversity of various regions and cultures throughout India.

Foods of north India

North Indian cuisine possibly influences Indian restaurant cuisine more than any other. A region that enjoys a temperate climate and rich fertile soils, its cuisine is the product of Punjabi and Mughal influences, characterized by the daily consumption of dairy foods: milk, paneer, ghee, cream (*malai*) and yogurt.

North Indian cuisine is recognized by the use of the *tava* (a cast-iron griddle) for cooking flat breads like roti and paratha, made from locally grown wheat and sometimes corn (maize) and eaten with every meal. Rice is not easily grown in the climate of the region.

Northern India is also home to the *tandoor*. Used for baking breads such as tandoori roti, naan and kulcha and cooking meat dishes like tandoori chicken and seekh kebab, it has become a trademark of Indian restaurants. Other breads like poori and bhatoora are deep-fried in ghee or oil and are common at festive occasions and street stalls. The population of the region is largely vegetarian but goat and lamb are consumed by a relatively small number of nonvegetarians.

The samosa is a north Indian favorite and now common in other parts of India, Asia and the Middle East, and generally served as an appetizer in Indian restaurants. The original samosa was filled with boiled, fried or mashed

potato and spices, but other tasty fillings have evolved and now include minced lamb or vegetables. Growing up I can remember making mountains of samosas from scratch for parties and festive occasions — no mean feat by any stretch of the imagination. Now you can buy them freshly cooked in any quantity from Indian stores and cafés. Generally, they are not as good as homemade but I am probably more pedantic than most.

Foods of south India

South Indian cooking boasts the value and versatility of rice as a staple food. The foods of southern India are often more fiery and pungent due to the liberal use of hot red chilies and souring ingredients like tamarind, kokum and lime. Coconut and curry leaves are also used liberally in this region and emerge in various tasteful guises at almost every meal. Cooks in this part of India tend to use spice pastes, moistened with water or oil, while in the north dishes are more often based on dry spice mixes such as garam masala. Some popular dishes include a varied range of biryanis and pilafs made with locally produced rice.

Foods of west India

Western India has three or four quite distinct food styles, the best known of which is probably Goan, a fusion of local and Portuguese cuisine. The Portuguese, who lived in the area for nearly 500 years, are the major influencers of the cuisine enjoyed up and down the west coast of India. The chili, which has become synonymous with Indian cuisine, was first introduced to India by the Portuguese. Rice is the staple grain and there is abundant use of fresh coconut and seafood flavored with fresh herbs and spice mixtures. Other regions in western India rely more on wheat, corn and maize for staples and use groundnut instead of coconut to add texture and thickness to dishes. To the north of the region, the predominantly vegetarian cuisine of Gujerat has its own distinctive character. Jaggery (boiled-down sugarcane juice) is often used to add sweetness and balance to the pungently spicy staples such as chili-flecked lentils, and tamarind is used to add a sour tang to vegetable dishes. Turmeric, chilies, cumin and cilantro are typically grown in the Gujerat.

Foods of east India

East Indian cuisine is famous for its desserts (*mathai*), particularly milk-based desserts such as the luscious *gulab jamon*, *rasgulla* and *chumchum*. Many of the desserts now popular in northern India originated in this region.

Cashew-nut, mustard-seed or poppy-seed pastes are used for thickening and are definitive of savory dishes in this part of India, whereas in other regions onions, ginger and garlic mixtures are used to flavor and thicken curry sauces. Fish and seafood are abundant and popular in the coastal states. Smaller fish are made into delicious, spicy soups or deep-fried and eaten with spicy pickles, sauces and chutneys. Larger fish are smothered and marinated with fragrant spice pastes before being lightly steamed or panfried.

- **Coriander leaves** — Coriander leaves (also called cilantro) and coriander seeds are quite dissimilar in taste, although if you pick the seeds while still green they have an intense coriander flavor. The distinct flavor of fresh leaves is incomparable for flavor and aroma. Fresh coriander leaves ground to a paste alone or with mint leaves are a popular base for fresh chutneys. Buy coriander from Indian grocers for a better-quality, less-expensive product, or grow your own for maximum flavor and freshness. Coriander leaves will be referred to as cilantro for this book.
- **Curry leaves** — Bright green, aromatic leaves that impart a "curryish" flavor to dishes. Use fresh or dried. Available from ethnic grocers, curry leaves freeze really well.
- **Fenugreek leaves** — Much more robust in flavor and aroma than coriander, fenugreek leaves are a tasty addition to bhajis, pakoras and curries. Fresh fenugreek leaves are readily available from Indian grocers, or can easily be grown from seed. *Kasoori methi* is sun-dried fenugreek and is a good substitute when fresh fenugreek is not available.
- **Fresh ginger** — Although dried ground ginger is used in a few traditional Indian dishes, it's more usual to cook with fresh gingerroot. Look for firm, unwrinkled roots.
- **Chilies** — Chilies come in many shapes, sizes and colors, and vary in heat from quite mild to extremely hot. Generally, the smaller the chili, the hotter it will be. Indian cooks and chefs mostly use fresh green chilies, the red ones being reserved for pickling or drying and pounding to chili powder. Chilies are easy to grow. Handle cut chilies carefully as the irritant in them causes a burning sensation on contact with the skin.
- **Chat masala** — The most popular and commonly used spice mix for Indian refreshments and snacks, this is a mix of roasted cumin and coriander seeds, chili, ground black peppercorns, ambchoor, salt and black salt (*sanchal*). Available in small packs from Indian grocers.
- **Ghee** — Ghee is clarified butter. It can be heated to a high temperature without burning and was traditionally prized and used for all cooking, sweet and savory. Nowadays it is

generally used only at special celebrations such as wedding feasts and religious occasions. Vegetable ghee is often used by Indian restaurant chefs but lacks the flavor of the real thing. At home, sunflower, olive or non-genetically modified canola oil is the preferred cooking medium for everyday meals, and is a healthier option.

■ **Chickpea flour (besan)** — Chickpea flour is used for bhajis, pakoras, yogurt-based curries and sweetmeats (confections or candies). Best purchased from Indian grocers.

■ **Jaggery** — Raw, unrefined sugar with a distinctive taste made from cooked-down sugarcane juice. Muscovado sugar or even dark brown sugar is fine as an alternative.

■ **Saffron** — Dried stigmas of crocus flowers, noted for its deep orange color and sweet, delicate aroma. Traditionally used in biryanis and other rice dishes. Needs to be soaked in water or milk before use.

■ **Tamarind** — A tart fruit used as a souring agent. Available in pods, blocks or as a concentrate. The concentrate is the most convenient but doesn't have the flavor and texture of the pods and blocks. If you plan to do a lot of cooking using tamarind, buy the block and soak in a little hot water for 20 minutes or so and squeeze out the pulp.

■ **Yogurt** — A cooling contrast to spicy dishes, and excellent for cleansing the palate after a hot curry. Homemade yogurt is superior in flavor to store-bought and is very easy to make. Recipe page 24.

■ **Atta** — Chapati flour is a finely ground, soft wheat flour with varying amounts of wheat bran, from dark wholemeal containing 100 percent of the bran to the lighter flours with large amounts of the bran removed. Canadian Gold, a new addition to the varieties of atta now available from Indian grocers, is a finely ground flour made from durum wheat and has a pale yellow tinge. The dough made from this flour doesn't need resting, so it is very convenient, but the chapatis don't keep as well. The lighter flours are generally used by restaurant chefs but I prefer the wholemeal for flavor and nutritional value.

■ **Basmati rice** — Basmati is the king of rice and Pakistani basmati rice considered to be the best. It has a nutty flavor and aroma and retains its "bite" when cooked. Use for savory and sweet dishes.

■ **Food coloring** — Red, yellow and green food coloring is used liberally by Indian chefs. Buy powdered colorings if you wish to use them or substitute with turmeric and paprika. You won't get the deep color of some of the restaurant dishes, but the flavor will not be affected.

■ **Oils** — Mustard-seed oil is widely used in India (and has been for centuries) for deep-frying and other cooking uses. The use of good-quality "healthy" oils, such as olive, safflower and non-genetically modified canola, will ensure that the food you enjoy is also contributing to good health. I use olive oil in most of my savory recipes as it has a fairly high cooking temperature and adds a nice taste, but this is a matter of personal choice.

Useful utensils

There are a few items of kitchen hardware that make preparing Indian restaurant food easier, less time consuming and more authentic:

■ A deep, heavy-bottomed frying pan or two needs to be at the top of your list. This enables the curries to be cooked quickly without burning and with even evaporation for thickening the sauces. It can also be used for making chapatis and parathas instead of using a tava (cast-iron griddle).

■ An upright blender is essential if you intend to make the curry sauce on a regular basis. A hand blender will suffice for small quantities although the sauce will not be quite as smooth.

■ A coffee grinder for grinding spices is also a good idea, unless you are skilled with a pestle and mortar.

■ A small pestle and mortar is useful for crushing whole spices such as whole cardamoms or coriander seeds.

■ A sizzle plate or two is a must if you like the tandoori dishes served sizzling at the table. You can make do with a cast-iron frying pan if you already have one and if you don't need to impress at the table.

■ A couple of balti dishes will add to the authenticity if you like balti curries.

■ A karahi or wok is useful, particularly if you want to cut down on the amount of oil used. Because of the pan's small base, the cooking oil sits in a small pool at the bottom, so you can use a lot less. It is also a good utensil for deep-frying foods such as samosas, pakoras, pooris and bhatooras (breads).

Handy tips, useful shortcuts and tricks of the trade

■ If you don't use up the fresh ginger, chilies and garlic that you have bought, place them all in your blender or food processor and process until fine. Freeze the mixture in ice-cube trays. Use a cube or two straight from the freezer when required.

■ Fresh green fenugreek left over from a bunch or a good harvest does not have to be wasted. Wash and dry well, chop and freeze in freezer bags or plastic containers. It doesn't turn into a solid mass, and you can use a little or a lot whenever you want, straight from the freezer.

■ Making samosas and don't want to take the time making and rolling the dough? Use wonton wrappers, spring-roll wrappers or even ready-made puff pastry instead. The result will not be authentic but it is a quick and tasty alternative.

■ Buy ready-made paneer or try tofu as a substitute. Both are available in blocks from supermarkets and health food stores.

■ Make a double quantity of chapati or naan dough, let it rest for 10–15 minutes and freeze half. Defrost in the fridge overnight when needed, and it will be as good as new.

- Save time by precooking diced vegetables such as carrots and potatoes in boiling salted water or the microwave for a few minutes, until almost tender. Use to make a speedy vegetable bhaji.
- Buy cauliflower when it is in season and cheap, break into florets and wash and drain. Blanch the florets in a large pot of boiling salted water for 2 minutes, drain and immediately immerse in ice cold water to stop the cooking process and maintain a nice color. Freeze in freezer bags. You can make aloo gobi or pakoras in a matter of minutes whenever you want. Restaurant chefs often use frozen cauliflower for speed and convenience.
- Save a little of your tandoori marinade and stir a tablespoon or so into your curries during the last minute or two of cooking for extra flavor and color.
- "Dry" popadoms, after frying in hot oil, upright (in a toast rack or metal colander) in a warm oven for a crisp, nongreasy result.
- Freeze quantities of the curry sauce, chicken and meat, cooked as suggested, and you can put your favorite curries together in minutes whenever you feel like having Indian food.

GET READY — IN SUMMARY

a) Make a small quantity of garam masala.

b) Prepare ground coriander and cumin.

c) Prepare garlic, ginger and chilies.

d) Have quantities of other essential and key ingredients to hand.

e) Make a quantity of curry sauce (page 32) and freeze it.

a) Garam masala

Garam means "hot" and *masala* a "mixture of spices." According to the Ayurvedic concept of health, food items have differing effects on our bodies and our health due to our constitution or *tri-dosha*. The heat from this "hot" spice mix is not a heat that you taste as with chilies, but one that warms the body. Spices such as cloves, cinnamon, black cardamoms and nutmeg are the garam constituents of this aromatic mixture.

b) Prepare ground coriander and cumin

Many recipes call for the use of coriander and cumin powder. Having the spices ground and ready to use makes life a lot easier.

GARAM MASALA

Makes about 3 tablespoons

1 tbsp coriander seeds
1 tbsp cumin
1 tsp green cardamoms
1 tsp cloves
1 tsp black peppercorns
2 sticks of cinnamon, about 2 inches (5 cm) in length
2 bay leaves
1/2 small nutmeg
4 black cardamoms

Place all the ingredients into an electric coffee grinder and grind to a fine powder. Carefully remove the lid and test by rubbing a little of the mixture between your forefinger and thumb. Finely ground spices should not feel gritty. If necessary, grind for another few seconds. Alternatively, grind to a fine powder in a pestle and mortar.

Store the ground spices in a small noncorrosive, airtight container and remember to label it.

Place 2 or 3 tablespoons of coriander seeds into the bowl of a coffee grinder and grind to a fine powder. Store in a small airtight container and label. Repeat with 2 or 3 tablespoons of cumin seeds.

c) Prepare garlic, ginger and chilies

Many of the dishes in this book require the use of finely chopped garlic, ginger and green chilies. If you plan to do much Indian cooking, it is helpful to have a quantity of these ready prepared so that you can put a meal together with the maximum of ease.

d) Have quantities of the other essential and key ingredients to hand

Ingredients such as turmeric, chili powder, paprika, cardamom pods, cinnamon and cloves are common items in Indian restaurant cooking. Have small amounts available at all times to make preparing your favorite dishes easy.

e) Make a quantity of curry sauce and freeze it

The basis for many of the curries in this book, the curry sauce makes preparing curries simplicity itself. See page 32 for this no-smell curry sauce.

GARLIC, GINGER AND CHILIES

Separate the cloves from 2 bulbs of garlic and peel.

Peel 11 oz (300 g) fresh ginger and roughly chop.

Place the garlic cloves and ginger in a food processor or blender and process until finely chopped.

Take an ice-cube tray and put 2 teaspoons of the mixture into each section.

Freeze until solid.

Remove the cubes of mix and place in a freezer bag or plastic container and store in the freezer.

One cube is approximately equivalent to 2 cloves of garlic and a 1-inch (2.5 cm) piece of ginger, the quantity and proportions used in most recipes, and can be used straight from the freezer or thawed in the microwave.

Green chilies — Repeat the above process with a quantity of green chilies. You probably require only half a cube of chilies for most recipes, but how much you use will depend on how hot the chilies are. Start with less, and add more if you want more heat.

6. WEIGHTS AND MEASURES

Both imperial and metric measurements have been given in this book with the imperial measures having been rounded up or down to the nearest unit. Remember to use one or the other and not to combine imperial and metric measurements in one recipe.

All spoon measurements throughout the book are **slightly rounded** spoonfuls unless specified as being level.

Fluid ounces refer to the British fluid ounce, which is slightly smaller than the US equivalent. This difference is not significant for the recipes in this book.

Cup size is half a US pint or the metric cup (250 mL).

Some conversions are given in the tables below:

MEASURE	USA	UK	AUSTRALIA
teaspoon	4.9 mL	5 mL	5 mL
dessertspoon	—	10 mL	10 mL
tablespoon	14.8 mL	15 mL	20 mL
cup	236.6 mL	285 mL	250 mL (metric cup)
fluid ounce	29.6 mL	28.4 mL	28.4 mL
liter	2.1 pints	2.2 pints	1000 mL

KILOGRAMS, POUNDS AND OUNCES

1 ounce (abbreviated oz) = approximately 28 g
1 lb (16 oz) = approximately 453 g
1 kilogram = 2 lb 4 oz
500 grams = 1 lb 2 oz

7.

THE NEW CURRY SAUCE

THIS IS the foundation of many of the curries served in Indian restaurants and is prepared in abundance and regularity by Indian chefs. Its recipe and method of preparation is also the most closely guarded secret of restaurant cooking. Indian cooking does not employ thickeners such as flour or cornstarch; it instead relies upon onions, ginger and garlic to give the sauce its substance, flavor and texture.

If you have purchased preparations of curry sauces from supermarkets or grocers and have been grossly disappointed with the end result, this recipe will be manna from heaven. This is the real thing. Have some of this curry sauce on hand, and you can prepare a delicious Indian meal in minutes, just like the experts.

The curry sauce is simple to make, and this method of making it, although different from the way it is made in many restaurants, smells pleasant during cooking. It keeps for up to four days in the fridge and can be frozen in serving-size portions for ultimate convenience.

These quantities make enough curry sauce for about eight main-course dishes.

Preparation and cooking time: about 1½ hours	4 tbsp olive oil 2 lb 4 oz (1 kg) onions, sliced 1 tsp salt about 2 oz (50 g) fresh ginger, coarsely chopped 2 oz (50 g) garlic, coarsely chopped	53 fl oz/3 US pints (1.5 L) water 1 can (8 oz/225 g) tomatoes 1 tsp tomato paste 1 tsp turmeric 1 tsp paprika

Step 1

■ Heat all but 1 tablespoon of the oil in a large saucepan with a tight-fitting lid, and add the sliced onions. Stir on high heat for a minute or two and then turn the heat down a little. Continue to cook the onion, stirring frequently, for about 10 minutes until the onion is transparent and beginning to brown at the edges.

■ Add the salt, stir well and turn the heat down to as low as you can. Cover the pan and continue to cook the onion for about 20 minutes, stirring three or four times during that period.

The addition of salt will prevent the onion from browning and help it soften and break down, but be careful it does not stick to the bottom of the pan.

■ Add the ginger and garlic to the onion. Turn the heat up a little and cook for a minute or two, until aromatic.

■ Add the water and bring to a boil. Turn the heat down and simmer the mixture, partly covered, for 20–25 minutes.

■ Leave to cool.

Step 2

■ Once cooled, ladle half the mixture into a blender and blend until smooth. To ensure that the sauce is really smooth, blend for about 2 minutes. Pour the blended onion mixture into a clean bowl and repeat with the other half of the onion mixture.

■ Wash and dry the saucepan. Reserve about 4 tablespoons of the sauce at this point to use for cooking the meat, as detailed in many of the recipes in this book.

Freezing: Freeze at this stage if you want to keep the sauce for up to 2 months. You can freeze the finished sauce for up to 1 month.

Step 3

■ Place the contents of the can of tomatoes into the rinsed blender and blend until smooth, about 2 minutes.

■ Place the cleaned saucepan onto medium heat and heat the remaining oil. Add the tomato paste, turmeric and paprika and cook for about 30 seconds. Add the blended tomatoes and bring to a boil. Turn down the heat and cook, stirring occasionally, for about 10 minutes.

■ Add the blended onion mixture to the tomatoes and bring to a boil again. Turn down the heat so that the sauce simmers gently.

■ As the sauce simmers, you will notice froth rises to the surface. This needs to be skimmed off. Continue to simmer, skimming as necessary, for 20–25 minutes.

■ Use immediately or cool and refrigerate for up to 4 days. Freeze for up to 1 month.

TIP

If you wish to speed things up a little, you can eliminate step 3. Simply add the spices, tomato paste and canned tomatoes to the onions in step 1, just before adding the water. Simmer for about 10 minutes before adding the water and proceed as suggested. Beware, though, that your blender will take on the yellow color of the turmeric. This will wash off more easily if you use a little dishwasher powder or laundry detergent dissolved in hot water.

8. APPETIZERS AND LIGHT LUNCHES

THE RICHNESS and diversity of Indian food are no more adequately reflected than in the enormous array of snacks, appetizers, hors d'oeuvres and tasty little tidbits enjoyed by millions of Indians every day. Each region of India has its own local specialities, but they are all tantalizingly spicy, delicious, inexpensive and readily available.

A variety of particularly common and popular snacks eaten throughout India are referred to as *chats*. Chana chat masala, chicken chat and aloo chat are all chats served in Indian restaurants, but there are many more varieties. They offer a hot, tangy and sweet mix of tastes that once acquired is forever desired.

The majority of traditional snacks are potato based. The aloo ki tikki for example, one of the oldest Indian snacks recorded in history, is made from mashed, spiced potatoes.

THE SAMOSA
Another popular snack, and one reportedly enjoyed by the British during the Raj, is the ubiquitous spicy little pastry triangle know as the samosa. It is believed that the samosa originated in central Asia before the 10th century and made its way to India via ancient trade routes such as the Old Silk Road. The samosa is now a popular snack all over the world.

Traditionally, samosas were made with potatoes, spices and vegetables. Modern-day Indian cuisine incorporates meat, fish and cheese into some of the original samosa recipes.

MAKING SAMOSAS FROM SCRATCH
A common practice not all that long ago, it is now a rarity to make samosas at home. And it's no wonder: it's a time- and effort-consuming task, particularly when making large amounts. Recipes and methods of preparation vary slightly from one household to another but all require the following steps:

- preparing and cooking the potato or meat filling
- preparing the pastry dough
- rolling the pastry
- filling the pastry
- deep-frying

Freshly made samosas are available readily and cheaply from Indian snack and sweet stores, and the vast majority of people, including many restaurant chefs, take the route of least inconvenience and buy them ready-made. However, the quality can be inconsistent. Homemade samosas are generally the best.

Serving Indian snacks and appetizers
Traditionally, there is no proper or right way to serve Indian food, although in Indian restaurants in the West it is common to eat two or more "courses." The dishes on the next pages can be served as appetizers if you wish to introduce a little formality into your occasion, or may form part of the main meal with a selection of dishes on the table at the same time. They also make delicious snacks at any time of the day. The important thing is to cook good food and enjoy it with family and friends.

Nonvegetarian appetizers

Lamb Boti
Chunks of tender lamb marinated in a mix of fresh ginger, garlic, chili and lemon juice.

Meat Samosa with Kashmiri Chat
Spicy minced lamb wrapped in a crisp light pastry served with chickpeas in a tamarind sauce.

Spicy Lamb Cutlets
Garlicky, spicy lamb cutlets marinated in fresh herbs and grilled until sizzling.

Kashmiri Lamb Cutlets
Meltingly tender lamb cutlets wrapped in a crisp, spicy golden coating.

Murgh Seekh Kebab
Minced chicken combined with fresh cilantro, spring onions, herbs and spices.

Murgh Tikka Hariyali
Tender breast pieces marinated in mint, green chilies and spices.

Chicken Dosai
Mustard-flavored shredded chicken wrapped in thin golden rice pancakes.

Fish Pakora
Pieces of fresh fish dipped in a chickpea-flour batter flavored with spices and herbs.

Ajwaini Jumbo Shrimp
Jumbo shrimp tossed with carom seeds, cilantro and cumin served with chargrilled orange slices.

LAMB BOTI

Traditionally, this dish uses cubed leg of lamb, marinated in spices and yogurt that tenderize and flavor the meat. It is then skewered and cooked over hot coals (or in the tandoor), creating lovely crispy pieces on the outside of the meat while the inside is deliciously moist and tender. You can achieve similar results on a barbecue, or failing that, a really hot oven or grill will be fine.

SERVES 4 Preparation and cooking time: 25–30 minutes (meat requires marinating overnight)	12 oz (350 g) lean lamb taken from the leg
	2 cloves of garlic, minced or finely chopped
	small piece of ginger, grated
	    (or a portion of prepared garlic-and-ginger
	    mix, page 30, thawed)
	1 tbsp chopped cilantro
	1/2 tsp turmeric
	1/2 tsp ground coriander
		1/2 tsp ground cumin
		1/2 tsp garam masala
		1 tsp chili powder
		juice of half a lemon or lime
		2 tbsp yogurt
		1 tbsp oil
		1 tsp salt

■ Cut the lamb into 1-inch (2.5 cm) chunks, place in a deep bowl and sprinkle on all the remaining ingredients except the yogurt, oil and salt.

■ Stir and turn the meat pieces until evenly coated with herbs and spices. Add the yogurt and oil and mix well. Cover and marinate the meat overnight in the fridge.

■ If you are using the oven, preheat it to 450°F (230°C). You may also consider using the barbecue or grill. Remove the meat from the fridge about 30 minutes before cooking.

■ Sprinkle the salt onto the meat and mix well. Thread the meat onto metal skewers (or presoaked wooden skewers), keeping the meat pieces about 1/2 inch (1 cm) apart. Reserve the marinade.

■ Cook the lamb in the oven for about 20–25 minutes, or on the barbecue or under the grill for about 15 minutes, turning once and brushing with the marinade halfway through cooking.

■ Serve with a crisp green salad and Yogurt Mint Sauce (page 40).

MEAT SAMOSA WITH KASHMIRI CHAT

This can be served as a hearty appetizer, a tasty snack with drinks or a light lunch. The fresh-tasting Kashmiri Chat incorporates sweet, hot and sour flavors and goes particularly well with these spicy samosas.

MAKES 12 SAMOSAS	5 oz (150 g) plain flour
Preparation and cooking time: 45 minutes (with ready-prepared filling)	1/2 tsp salt
	1 tbsp olive oil
	about 4 fl oz (120 mL) water
	1 quantity of Karahi Keema (page 96)
	oil for deep-frying

■ To make the pastry dough, sift the flour and salt into a bowl. Make a well in the center of the flour and add the oil.

■ Add the water, a little at a time starting at the center to incorporate the oil, and mix, bringing the flour together until you have a soft, pliable dough.

■ Knead gently for a minute or two. Cover and leave to rest for about 10 minutes.

■ Divide the mixture into 6 portions. Take one portion and roll between floured hands to make a ball. Flatten slightly and roll into a circle about 8 inches (20 cm) in diameter.

■ Cut each circle in half, and then taking the two corners of one half, bring the cut sides together, slightly overlapping, to make a hollow cone. Seal by pressing the cut sides together. You may need to dampen the edges with a little water.

■ Fill about three-quarters full with the Karahi Keema mixture, being careful not to overfill. Pinch the open ends together firmly to close. Set aside and repeat with remaining dough.

■ Deep-fry in batches and drain on a wire rack. Keep warm in a low oven while cooking the remaining samosas.

Kashmiri Chat

1 heaped tsp tamarind paste
about 3 fl oz (100 mL) water
1 can (15 oz/425 g) chickpeas, drained
1 small red onion, finely diced
1 tomato, deseeded and the flesh diced
1 green chili, finely chopped
1 tsp Kashmiri chili powder, or $\frac{1}{2}$ tsp red chili powder
$\frac{1}{2}$ tsp garam masala
1 tsp chat masala
1 tsp salt
1 tbsp ketchup
1 tbsp chopped cilantro

Dissolve the tamarind in the water and place all the other ingredients in a bowl. Mix well.

If you are using a block of tamarind for the Kashmiri Chat, soak a golf-ball-sized piece in 4 fl oz (120 mL) of hot water for 20–30 minutes. Squeeze out the pulp and discard solids and seeds.

Note: Kashmiri chili powder is redder but milder than ordinary chili powder.

TIP

Make the chat the day before and allow the flavors to develop.

SPICY LAMB CUTLETS

These lamb cutlets are so succulent and tasty you will have everyone coming back for more. The cutlets come from the rib and contain the tender fillet attached to the rib bone which makes them ideal as a finger food for informal gatherings.

SERVES 4

Preparation and cooking time: approximately 30 minutes (plus 2–3 hours marinating time)

8 lamb cutlets
2 tbsp finely chopped mint leaves (or 2 heaped tsp mint jelly out of a jar)
1 tsp chili powder
1 tsp paprika
3 cloves of garlic, minced or finely chopped
1 tsp ground cumin

1 tsp ground coriander
juice of half a lemon
1 tbsp olive oil
1 tbsp mint jelly
1 tsp salt

- Trim the cutlets and scrape the bone ends to remove fat and gristle.

- Mix all the remaining ingredients except the salt in a bowl, and add the lamb cutlets. Using your hands, rub the herb-and-spice mixture onto the meat ensuring each cutlet is evenly coated. Cover and leave to marinate in the fridge for at least 2 hours or overnight.

- Remove the lamb from the fridge about half an hour before cooking.

- Heat a heavy-based frying pan, capable of holding the cutlets without overcrowding, until very hot.

- Sprinkle some salt onto each cutlet. Cook the cutlets for about 1$^{1}/_{2}$ minutes each side.

- Serve hot with Yogurt Mint Sauce.

YOGURT MINT SAUCE

5 fl oz (150 mL) plain yogurt
1 tsp mint sauce
$^{1}/_{2}$ level tsp salt
$^{1}/_{4}$ tsp chili powder
$^{1}/_{4}$ tsp garam masala
$^{1}/_{4}$ tsp green mango powder
$^{1}/_{2}$ tsp finely granulated sugar
2 tsp chopped fresh mint (optional)

Place all the ingredients in a bowl and mix well.

TIPS

The mint jelly is the secret ingredient in this dish. The hint of sweetness balances the lemon juice and spices beautifully.

Ready-prepared garlic, usually preserved in lemon juice, is also a good shortcut for marinades requiring lots of garlic.

KASHMIRI LAMB CUTLETS

This is an unusual but absolutely delicious dish of precooked, tender lamb cutlets, wrapped in a golden, crispy batter.

SERVES 4 Preparation and cooking time: 45–50 minutes	8 lamb cutlets 7 fl oz (200 mL) milk 1/2 tsp garam masala 3 cloves 6 cardamom pods 1 tsp grated ginger 1 tbsp chopped onion sprinkling of salt	3 tbsp chickpea flour (besan) 1 tbsp rice flour 1 tsp chili powder 1/2 tsp paprika 1/2 tsp salt 1/2 tsp turmeric 1/4 tsp ground fenugreek leaves (optional) oil for deep-frying

Step 1

■ Trim the cutlets and scrape the bone end of each cutlet. Place the milk, garam masala, cloves, cardamoms, ginger and onion in a pan large enough to hold the cutlets in a single layer, and bring to a boil.

■ Add the cutlets, bring the milk back to a boil, turn down the heat and simmer gently for about 20 minutes, turning once or twice, until the cutlets are tender and all the liquid has evaporated.

■ Sprinkle the cutlets with a little salt on each side, remove from the pan and cool.

■ Cutlets can be prepared to this stage up to 24 hours ahead.

Step 2

■ Combine the chickpea flour, rice flour, chili powder, paprika, salt, turmeric and fenugreek leaves (if you are using them) in a bowl. Add enough water to make a thickish batter. Allow to stand for at least 10 minutes.

■ Dip the lamb cutlets in the batter, shaking off the excess, and fry in hot oil until crisp and golden.

■ Drain on paper towels and serve with spicy Peach Chutney (page 172) or Yogurt Mint Sauce (page 40).

TIP

The rice flour helps to make the batter crispier but it is not essential. Use extra chickpea flour if you don't have it.

MURGH SEEKH KEBAB

Made with lean minced chicken and fresh herbs, these tasty kebabs make a nice change from the traditional lamb seekh kebabs.

SERVES 4		
Preparation and cooking time: 20–25 minutes	2 spring onions, finely sliced 2 tbsp chopped cilantro 2 green chilies, finely chopped 2 tsp fresh ginger, grated 3 cloves of garlic, finely chopped	8 oz (225 g) minced chicken 1 tsp salt 1 tsp garam masala juice of half a lemon 1 egg, lightly beaten

BE A SIZZLER

- Heat a sizzle plate on a gas flame for about 5 minutes until very hot.
- Turn down the heat and place some sliced onion onto the dish.
- Immediately place the cooked food on top of the onion.
- Drizzle a little oil onto the side of the dish and tilt it slightly so the oil runs across the dish. It will start sizzling.
- Now move some of the food aside and drizzle some lemon juice onto the onions. This produces even more sizzling and a delicious aroma.
- Finally, sprinkle with chopped cilantro, and serve.

■ Preheat the oven to its maximum temperature, or turn on the grill to heat. Place all the ingredients into a large bowl, and using your hands mix thoroughly.

■ Divide the mixture into 8 equal parts, and using oiled hands form into sausage shapes about 4 inches (10 cm) in length.

■ Place these on a rack in a shallow baking tray and cook near the top of the oven for 10–12 minutes, or under a very hot grill for 8–10 minutes, turning once.

■ Serve sizzling with a green salad, Yogurt Mint Sauce (page 40) and a wedge of lemon.

TIP

Place the first five ingredients, roughly chopped, into the bowl of a small food processor and process for a few seconds until finely chopped. Combine with the remaining ingredients and proceed as above.

MURGH TIKKA HARIYALI

Chicken tikka with fresh green (*hariyali*) herbs appears to be a Bengali dish, although the Punjabis also claim it as their own. Beautifully spiced, aromatic with fresh herbs, it will stimulate your tastebuds and your appetite. It's easy to prepare and very tasty.

SERVES 4–6

Preparation and cooking time: 30 minutes (plus marinating time of 2–3 hours or overnight)

3 chicken fillets
juice of half a lemon or lime
1 tsp salt
3 tbsp cilantro
3 tbsp mint leaves
4 or 5 fresh curry leaves
3 or 4 green garlic tops (optional)

2 green chilies
1-inch (2.5 cm) piece of ginger, roughly chopped
2 cloves of garlic, roughly chopped
1 tsp garam masala
2 tbsp yogurt
1 tbsp oil plus extra for basting

■ Rinse the chicken fillets, pat dry with paper towels, and cut into 1 1/2-inch (4 cm) chunks. Sprinkle the lemon or lime juice and salt onto the chicken, stir well and set aside.

■ Place the herbs, chilies, ginger, garlic, garam masala, yogurt and oil into a blender or food processor and process to a coarse paste.

■ Add the herb paste to the chicken, mix well and refrigerate for 2–3 hours or overnight to marinate.

■ Remove the chicken from the fridge at least half an hour before cooking and insert onto metal or presoaked wooden skewers.

■ Heat the grill or barbecue and cook the chicken skewers for 12–15 minutes, basting once or twice with a little oil and turning frequently until cooked through.

■ Serve hot with Mango Chutney (page 171) and lemon wedges.

TIP

You can brown the chicken pieces in a very hot frying pan, then, using kitchen tongs, skewer them and bake in a hot oven at 425°F (220°C) for 15 minutes.

CHICKEN DOSAI

The dosai, or dosa as it is commonly known in the West, originates from south India although it is popular all over the country. Dosai are made from a batter of soaked, ground and fermented rice and urad dhal, which is poured onto a tava (cast-iron griddle) and fried in oil or ghee, rather like a pancake or crepe. Traditionally dosai are served with a variety of chutneys and eaten for breakfast. In the West it is more usual to eat dosai stuffed with spicy potato or meat fillings, more commonly referred to as masala dosai.

Making the dosai batter at home is a lengthy and laborious process. The quick and convenient way is to buy the ready-prepared mix, which is very good and available from Indian grocers. Simply add the filling of your choice. Making dosai takes a little practice, so be prepared to throw the first couple away. Starting with a warm rather than hot pan makes it easier, and practice makes perfect.

SERVES 4

Preparation and cooking time: approximately 45 minutes

2 tbsp olive oil
1 tsp black mustard seeds
2 onions, sliced
4 or 5 curry leaves, fresh or dried
2 cloves of garlic, finely chopped
1-inch (2.5 cm) piece of ginger, finely chopped (or a portion of prepared garlic-and-ginger mix, page 30, thawed)

2–3 green chilies, finely sliced
1 tsp salt
1/2 tsp turmeric
8 oz (225 g) chicken, thinly sliced
1 tsp garam masala
1 tbsp cilantro
1 pkt of dosai mix
about 2 tbsp oil extra

■ Heat the oil in a medium saucepan. When hot, throw in the mustard seeds, shake the pan for 2 or 3 seconds until they pop and quickly add the onions followed by the curry leaves.

■ Cook on medium to high heat until the onions are translucent and add the garlic, ginger and chilies. Stir-fry for a minute or two.

■ Add the salt and turmeric, stir and add in the chicken. Continue stirring on medium to high heat until the chicken begins to color.

■ Add 4 tablespoons of water, cover the pan, turn down the heat and cook for 10 minutes, stirring occasionally.

SAMBHAR

1/2 tsp fenugreek seeds
1/2 tsp coriander seeds
1/2 tsp cumin seeds
1/2 tsp black peppercorns
6 dried red chilies
3 tsp tamarind paste
7 fl oz (200 mL) warm water
7 oz (200 g) red lentils
7 oz (200 g) chopped mixed vegetables
1/2 tsp turmeric
18 fl oz (500 mL) cold water
1 tbsp oil
1/2 tsp black mustard seeds
8 curry leaves
1 medium onion, chopped
pinch asafetida (optional)
1 ripe tomato, chopped
2 tsp salt (or to taste)
2 tbsp chopped cilantro

In a small pan dry-roast the fenugreek, coriander, cumin, peppercorns and chilies until aromatic. Remove from the pan, cool and grind to a powder.

Dissolve the tamarind in about 7 fl oz (200 mL) of warm water. Set aside.

Meanwhile, wash and drain the lentils and combine with the vegetables, turmeric and 18 fl oz (500 mL) of water. Bring to a boil, skim the froth off the top and simmer for 30 minutes, stirring now and then.

In a separate pan, heat the oil and add the mustard seeds and curry leaves. Cook for a minute and stir in the onion (and asafetida, if you are using it).

Stir-fry the onion until it starts to color and add the tamarind water. Bring to a boil and simmer for 5 minutes.

Add the onion mixture to the dhal (pulses) and vegetables with the tomato, salt and roasted spice mix. Bring back to a boil and simmer for another 5 minutes.

Stir in the cilantro and serve with dosai.

■ Remove the lid and cook on low heat for another 5 minutes until the mixture is dry and the chicken cooked.

■ Stir in the garam masala and cilantro.

■ For dosai, follow instructions on the packet to make the batter and allow to stand for 5 minutes. Set the oven to warm.

■ Warm a frying pan that is about 20–25cm (8–10 inches) in diameter and generously brush or spray with oil.

■ Pour a little batter into the pan and, using a circular motion, spread it around with the back of a spoon.

■ Cook on medium heat and, while the dosai cooks, sprinkle or spray some more oil onto the top and around the edges so that it seeps under the dosai. It will take around 4 minutes to cook.

■ When the edges start to brown, carefully lift the dosai onto an ovenproof platter. Place some filling along the center of the dosa, and fold over one side and then the other. Hold down for a few seconds to set the dosai in shape.

■ Place in the oven to keep warm while making more dosai.

■ Serve warm with Coconut and Mint Chutney (page 173) and Sambhar.

TIP

Have two pans going at the same time, so that you have a cooler one for starting each dosai. Take your time spreading the batter and don't worry if your dosai has large holes or spaces in it. The edges of these holes will get nice and crisp and make it taste even better.

FISH PAKORA

Succulent, creamy chunks of fish wrapped in spicy, crisp, golden batter; equally at home as a snack with ketchup or as an elegant appetizer with baby salad leaves, sweet chili sauce and a wedge of lime.

SERVES 4		
Preparation and cooking time: 25–30 minutes	4 oz (120 g) chickpea flour (besan) 1 oz (30 g) rice flour 1 tsp salt 1 green chili, finely chopped 1/2 tsp chili powder 1 heaped tsp mint sauce	1/2 tsp garam masala 1/2 tsp ground fenugreek leaves (optional) 8–10 oz (225–280 g) piece of firm white fish 1 tbsp finely chopped cilantro oil for deep-frying

- Sift the chickpea flour, rice flour and salt into a large bowl. Add enough water to make into a thick batter.

- Stir in the salt, chili and chili powder, mint sauce, garam masala and fenugreek leaves, if you are using them. Allow the batter to stand while preparing the fish.

- Rinse the fish, pat dry with paper towels, and cut into large chunks about 2 inches (5 cm) in size.

- Stir the cilantro into the batter, followed by the fish pieces. Stir the fish around in the batter until each piece is well coated.

- Shake off excess batter, and deep-fry the fish pieces in hot oil for 3–4 minutes until the coating is a rich golden brown and the fish is cooked through.

- Serve hot.

TIPS

Use any leftover batter to make vegetable pakora. Simply dip bite-sized pieces of cauliflower, potato, mushroom or eggplant into the batter and deep-fry until crisp. Or stir in some sliced onion or spinach, and drop spoonfuls into hot oil.

If you have some fresh fenugreek, stir it into the batter with the spices; it is wonderful in this dish.

Ajwaini Jumbo Shrimp

Jumbo shrimp are fished from various warm waters around the world and are available precooked, and "green" (raw) if you are fortunate enough to live close to fish markets. If buying frozen shrimp, allow plenty of time for defrosting. The best way of defrosting them is slowly in the fridge.

This is an impressive dish that is bursting with flavor. It is delicately yet distinctly spiced with the unique flavor of carom seeds (or ajowan seeds) and the tangy sweetness of the orange.

SERVES 4		
Preparation and cooking time: 30 minutes including marinating time	16 jumbo shrimp 1 tsp carom seeds (*ajwain*) 1 tsp ground cumin 1 tsp ground coriander 1/2 tsp turmeric 1 green chili, finely chopped	1 tbsp finely chopped cilantro 1 tsp olive oil zest of half an orange 1 tsp salt 1 orange, sliced

■ If using fresh shrimp, shell and devein them, leaving the tail intact. Rinse under cold water, drain and pat dry with paper towels.

■ Mix all the remaining ingredients, except for the salt and the sliced orange, in a noncorrosive bowl and add the shrimp. Stir to coat and leave to marinate for 15 minutes.

■ Heat a heavy-based frying pan large enough to take the shrimp in a single layer. Stir the salt into the shrimp, cook them over medium heat for about 5 minutes, turning once or twice.

■ Meanwhile, chargrill the orange slices on a griddle pan, a minute each side.

■ Serve the shrimp, sizzling if you like (see page 42), with a green salad, the chargrilled orange slices and Cilantro and Mint Drizzle.

Cilantro and Mint Drizzle

Take a handful of fresh cilantro and mint, one or two green chilies, juice of a lemon, 1 teaspoon of finely granulated sugar, and salt and pepper to taste, and place in a blender. Blend until smooth.

Vegetarian appetizers

Spinach Bhaji
Shredded spinach combined with chickpea flour, herbs and spices, deep-fried until golden.

Vegetarian Samosa
Spicy, tangy potatoes wrapped in a light, crisp pastry.

Vegetarian Dosai
Thin, golden rice pancakes filled with spiced mustard potatoes, served with a coconut (*nariyal*) and mint chutney.

Paneer Shashlik
Cubes of homemade cheese marinated with a blend of herbs and spices, cooked with onions and sweet peppers.

Spring Rolls
Spring-roll pastry filled with finely diced vegetables and paneer, lightly spiced and deep-fried until golden.

Aloo Ki Tikki
Crisp, golden potato patties, lightly spiced and flavored with fresh herbs. Served with a tamarind sauce.

Dhal Soup
A combination of vegetables and lentils in a mildly spiced soup.

SPINACH BHAJI

Spinach Bhaji, or palak pakorah as it is referred to in India, is just one of the many types of spicy snacks made with chickpea (besan) flour. It is quick, easy and tasty and in fact quite nutritious. A good appetizer or snack for vegetarians and nonvegetarians alike.

SERVES 4–6	8 oz (225 g) chickpea flour (besan)	2 tbsp tomato puree (optional)
	2 tsp salt	1 bunch (about 7 oz/200 g) spinach leaves
Preparation and cooking time: 20–25 minutes	1 tsp garam masala	oil for deep-frying
	1 or 2 green chilies, finely chopped (or half a portion of prepared chilies, page 30)	

■ Place all the ingredients except the spinach in a bowl and add enough water to make a thick batter. Cover and leave to stand while preparing the spinach.

■ Wash the spinach leaves in plenty of water, squeeze out excess water and shred the leaves finely. Add to the batter and stir well.

■ Deep-fry tablespoons of the mixture in hot oil. Do not overcrowd the pan. Press the bhaji lightly while it is frying to squeeze the uncooked mixture to the outside and ensure thorough cooking.

■ Drain on paper towels and serve hot with sauce or chutney of choice.

TIP

Use frozen, thawed spinach for added convenience.

VEGETARIAN SAMOSA

The ubiquitous samosa is a popular snack throughout India and famous around the world. A delightful crisp, deep-fried triangle with a delicious spicy filling, it is versatile enough for a quick snack on the run or as part of a prestigious banquet.

   The carrots used in this recipe give the filling added flavor and texture, but you can omit them and make up the quantity with more potato.

MAKES 12 SAMOSAS

Preparation and cooking time: filling: 25–30 minutes, pastry and remaining process: 40–45 minutes

Filling
2 oz (50 g) diced carrot
5 oz (150 g) diced potato
2 tbsp olive oil
1 onion, finely sliced
1-inch (2 cm) piece of ginger, grated or finely chopped
1 or 2 green chilies, finely chopped
1/2 tsp turmeric
1/2 tsp cumin seeds

1 tsp salt
3 tbsp frozen peas
1 tsp green mango powder or juice of half a lemon
1/2 tsp garam masala

Pastry
5 oz (150 g) plain flour
1/2 tsp salt
1 tbsp olive oil
4 fl oz (120 mL) water
oil for deep-frying

TAMARIND SAUCE

2 tsp tamarind paste
7 fl oz (200 mL) warm water
1/2 tsp salt
1/2 tsp chili powder
1/2 tsp garam masala
1/2 tsp green mango powder
1 tbsp ketchup
1 carrot, grated
1 tbsp diced red onion
1 tbsp chopped cilantro

Dissolve the tamarind paste in the water.

Add the remaining ingredients and mix to combine.

■ Make the filling first. Boil the carrot in salted water for 5 minutes and add the potato. Cook until the vegetables are tender but not breaking apart. Drain.

■ Meanwhile, heat the oil in a heavy-based saucepan and add the onion. Fry for a few minutes over medium heat until the onion is beginning to color around the edges.

■ Add the ginger, chilies, turmeric, cumin and salt and stir-fry for 2 minutes. Stir in the cooked vegetables, peas, green mango powder and garam masala. Mix well over low heat for a few minutes so that the vegetables absorb the spices.

■ Turn off the heat and allow the filling to cool while making the pastry.

■ To make the pastry dough, sift the flour and salt into a bowl. Make a well in the center of the flour and add the oil. Add about 4 fl oz (120 mL) of water, a little at a time starting at the center to incorporate the oil, and mix, bringing the flour together until you have a soft, pliable dough. Knead gently for a minute or two until smooth.

■ Cover and leave to rest for about 10 minutes.

■ With floured hands, divide the mixture into 6 portions. Take one portion and roll between floured hands to make a ball. Flatten slightly and roll into a thin circle about 8 inches (20 cm) in diameter.

■ Cut each circle in half and, taking the two corners of one half, bring the cut sides together, slightly overlapping, to make a hollow cone. Seal by pressing the cut sides together. You may need to dampen the edges with a little water.

■ Fill about three-quarters full with the potato mixture, being careful not to overfill. Pinch the open ends together firmly to enclose the filling. Set aside and repeat with the remaining dough.

■ Deep-fry in batches and drain on a wire rack. Keep warm in a low oven while cooking the remaining samosas.

■ Serve piping hot with Tamarind Sauce, Kashmiri Chat (page 39) or ketchup.

Vegetarian Dosai

This is a delicious and quite substantial dish with a lovely combination of textures and flavors: crispy pancake, moist filling, a fresh-tasting chutney and an earthy, tangy Sambhar (page 45). For some tips on making the dosai, see the Chicken Dosai recipe (page 44).

SERVES 4

Preparation and cooking time: 45 minutes

2 tbsp olive oil
1 tsp black mustard seeds
1 onion, sliced
4–5 curry leaves, fresh, frozen or dried
2 green chilies, finely chopped
1/2 tsp ground cumin

1/2 tsp ground coriander
1/2 tsp turmeric
1 1/2 tsp salt
11 oz (300 g) diced potato
1 pkt of dosai mix

■ Heat the oil in a heavy-based pan and add the mustard seeds. Shake the pan over the heat for a couple of seconds until the seeds pop and immediately add the onion and curry leaves.

■ Cook, stirring over medium to high heat, until the onion is translucent, about 5 minutes. Add the chilies, cumin, coriander, turmeric and salt. Stir for a few seconds until aromatic and add the potato.

■ Stir-fry the potato in the oil-and-spice mix for 3–4 minutes and add 3 tablespoons of water. Stir again, cover and allow to cook over low heat for about 10–15 minutes until the potato pieces are tender.

■ For the dosai, follow instructions on the packet to make the batter and allow to stand for 5 minutes. Set the oven to warm.

■ Gently warm a frying pan about 8–10 inches (20–25 cm) in diameter and generously brush or spray with oil. Pour a little batter into the pan and, using a circular motion, spread it around with the back of a spoon.

■ Cook on medium heat for about 4 minutes. While the dosai cooks, sprinkle or spray some oil onto the top and around the edges so that it seeps under the dosai.

■ When the edges start to brown, carefully lift the dosai onto an ovenproof plate. Place some filling along the center of the dosai, and fold over one side and then the other. Hold down for a few seconds and it will hold its shape.

■ Keep warm while making more dosai. Serve warm with Coconut and Mint Chutney (page 173) and Sambhar (page 45).

TIP

Have two pans going at the same time, so that you have a cool one for starting each dosai.

Paneer Shashlik

Paneer or curd is used for a variety of Indian dishes both sweet and savory, particularly in northern India. It is rich in protein, making it a good substitute for meat in vegetarian meals. This dish is a tasty and colorful appetizer.

SERVES 4		
Preparation and cooking time: 20–25 minutes (marinating time 2–3 hours)	8 oz (225 g) paneer (recipe page 24) 1 green pepper 1 red pepper 1 onion 2 firm tomatoes 5 fl oz (150 mL) plain yogurt 1/2 tsp salt 1 tsp turmeric	2 green chilies, finely chopped (or half a portion of prepared chilies, page 30) 1/2 tsp ground cumin 1/2 tsp ground black pepper 1 tbsp chopped cilantro 1 tbsp chopped mint juice of half a lemon 2 tbsp olive oil

■ Cut the paneer into even-sized chunks about 1 x 1 inch (2.5 x 2.5 cm). Cut the peppers into squares and the onion and tomatoes into large chunks, about the same size as the paneer.

■ Thread the paneer and vegetables onto 8 skewers (presoaked if you are using wooden ones), dividing the ingredients equally. Place in a shallow, nonmetallic dish that will hold the skewers in a single layer.

■ Place all the remaining ingredients and half the oil into a bowl and mix until combined. Pour the marinade over the skewers, turning each skewer until the paneer and vegetables are well coated with the marinade. Cover and refrigerate for 2 or 3 hours.

■ Remove the skewers from the fridge about half an hour before cooking and heat the grill or barbecue. Brush or spray the skewered ingredients with oil, and grill or barbecue on all sides for 3–4 minutes until the paneer and vegetables are charred around the edges.

■ Serve hot with a spicy salad and naan or chapati.

SPRING ROLLS

Although the filling is a little different, Indian spring rolls are similar to Chinese spring rolls in appearance, texture and taste, only much spicier. This is quite an easy recipe that is even easier if you use ready-made spring-roll pastry available from Asian grocers and supermarkets.

SERVES 4–6

Preparation and cooking time: 35–40 minutes

Filling
2 tbsp olive oil
2 cloves of garlic, minced or finely chopped
small piece of ginger, grated
    (or a portion of prepared garlic-and-ginger
    mix, page 30, thawed)
1 carrot, grated
1 green pepper, cut into thin strips

2 oz (50 g) cabbage, thinly sliced
2 oz (50 g) paneer (page 24), cut into small cubes
1$1/2$ tbsp soy sauce
Pastry
3 oz (100 g) plain flour
2 oz (50 g) cornstarch
1 small egg, beaten
oil for deep-frying

■ Heat the oil in a karahi or saucepan and add the garlic and ginger. Stir-fry for a minute or two and add all the remaining ingredients for the filling except for the paneer and soy sauce, and mix well.

■ Continue to stir-fry on medium heat for 5–6 minutes until the vegetables are tender crisp. Add a little water if required to prevent them from burning. Turn off the heat and stir in the paneer and soy sauce. Allow the vegetables to cool while making the pastry.

■ Sift the flour and cornstarch into a medium bowl; add the beaten egg and enough water to make a thickish batter. Do not overmix.

■ Heat a pancake pan, or nonstick frying pan, and brush or spray with a little oil. Pour in about 2 tablespoons of batter and spread thinly over the pan to make a thin pancake. Turn when the underside is lightly brown and brown the other side. Repeat with the remaining batter.

■ Place a pancake on a flat surface in front of you. Put about a tablespoon of vegetable filling onto the half nearest to you, about 1 inch (2.5 cm) from the edge. Fold this edge over the filling, fold over once more, then bring in the sides. Continue to roll tightly until you have a neat roll. Secure with a toothpick if necessary.

■ Repeat with the remaining filling and pancakes.

■ Deep-fry the rolls in hot oil until crisp and golden. Drain and serve with a sauce of your choice. Tamarind Sauce (page 50) or the Cilantro and Mint Drizzle (page 47) is delicious with these rolls.

ALOO KI TIKKI

A delicious snack any time of the day, Aloo Ki Tikki is a popular vegetarian appetizer in Indian restaurants. It is a tasty, spicy potato *tikki* (patty), panfried until golden and crispy. Serve it with an assortment of chutneys and sweet, sour or spicy sauces.

There are as many recipes for making these lovely little potato cakes as there are cooks. The one below is quick and easy.

SERVES 4–6 (MAKES 12 PATTIES) Preparation and cooking time: 35–40 minutes	8 oz (225 g) potatoes, peeled and cut into 　large chunks pat of butter 3 tbsp frozen peas 1/2 onion, finely chopped 1 tsp salt 1 tsp turmeric	1 tsp green mango powder 2 green chilies, finely chopped (or half a portion 　of prepared chilies, page 30) 1 tbsp chopped cilantro 1 tsp garam masala oil for pan frying

- Cook the potatoes in boiling salted water for about 15 minutes until tender. Drain well and return to the hot saucepan to dry off completely.

- Add the butter and mash the potato until smooth.

- Microwave or boil the peas until just cooked and add to the mashed potato with all the remaining ingredients except the oil. Mix well.

- Take about a tablespoon of mixture and, with oiled hands, roll first into a ball and then flatten slightly to make a patty. Repeat with the remaining potato mixture.

- Heat a heavy-based, nonstick frying pan and pour in enough oil to cover the base. Add the potato patties to the pan in batches and cook over low to medium heat for about 5 minutes each side until golden and crisp. Add a little more oil as required.

- Serve hot with Kashmiri Chat (page 39), Mango Chutney (page 171) or Tamarind Sauce (page 50).

TIP

For a lower-fat version, spray tikkies lightly with oil and bake in a hot oven at 425°F (220°C) for 20–25 minutes.

DHAL SOUP

A simple example of "fusion" cooking, this warming soup is simple to prepare and delicious to eat. You can use practically any combination of vegetables that are in season.

SERVES 6–8		
Preparation and cooking time: 1 hour 15 minutes	1 cob of sweet corn 1 onion 1 medium potato 1 medium carrot 1 stick of celery approx. 7 oz (200 g) butternut squash 2 ripe tomatoes, chopped 2 tbsp olive oil 1 tsp ground cumin	1 tsp ground coriander 1 tsp chili powder 3 tbsp red lentils, washed 70 fl oz/4.2 US pints (2 L) water 1 vegetable stock cube 2 tsp salt or to taste juice of a lime 1 tbsp chopped cilantro

- Remove husk and hairs from the corn and discard. Using a sharp knife, slice off the kernels. Peel and coarsely chop the remaining vegetables.

- Place all the vegetables in the bowl of a food processor and process briefly, or chop finely.

- Heat the oil in a large heavy-based saucepan and add the spices. Fry for a few seconds and stir in the vegetables.

- Stir-fry for about 2 minutes and add the lentils, water, stock cube (crumbled) and salt. Bring to a boil. Turn down the heat and skim the froth off the surface.

- Partly cover and simmer for about an hour, stirring once or twice. Stir in the lime juice and cilantro, and serve.

9. TANDOORI COOKING

WHO CAN possibly resist the delicious morsels of succulently tender meat and hot, puffy naan breads emerging from the flaming hot coals? With its origins in the north of India, the tandoor has taken up permanent residence in the West!

Used widely throughout Asia and the Middle East, there is evidence that the tandoor has been around for a very long time and was used by ancient civilizations since before the birth of Christ. It is constructed from clay and has a unique shape; wide at the bottom and narrowing to about a third of its width at the top.

The somewhat potbellied shape of the tandoor is sometimes referred to disparagingly by Indians to describe someone roundly obese or "tandoorlike."

The heat from the red-hot embers at the base of the tandoor is intensified by the narrowing shape and temperatures can reach as high as 896°F (480°C). The intense heat cooks food quickly, crisping it on the outside while maintaining a tender succulence on the inside. Meat and fish are skewered on *seekhs* (long metal skewers) and cooked by lowering the seekhs into the oven from the top and leaving them in the hot interior for a few minutes, the hooked ends of the seekhs hanging from bars placed at the mouth of the tandoor; breads are cooked by slapping them onto the inside wall. The tandoor is traditionally fired with charcoal although some of the modern ovens use electricity or gas.

The tandoor shares some similarities with the Italian wood-fired oven and the common barbecue, but its shape and the cooking techniques employed in its use make it unique. The extremely hot temperatures, the charcoal that fires it, and the flame-grilled flavor and crispness it imparts to cooked foods are difficult to replicate at home. Nevertheless good results can be achieved using a very hot oven, an effective grill or, if weather permits, a barbecue.

TANDOORI MARINADE

Apart from a tandoor, a good marinade and time are the key elements required for producing good "tandoori" dishes.

Makes approximately 11 fl oz (300 mL)
Preparation time: 5 minutes

10 fl oz (275 mL) plain yogurt
2 green chilies, roughly chopped
2 tsp grated ginger
3 cloves of garlic
1^1/$_2$ tsp salt
1 tsp red chili powder
1 tsp black cumin
1^1/$_2$ tsp garam masala
2 tsp vinegar
2 tbsp olive oil
^{1}/$_2$ tsp red food coloring or 2 tsp paprika
^{1}/$_2$ tsp yellow food coloring or 2 tsp turmeric

Combine the yogurt, green chilies, ginger and garlic in a blender until smooth.

Empty into a bowl and add all the remaining ingredients. Mix until well combined.

Tandoori dishes

Tandoori Chicken

Buy small birds no more than 2 lb 8 oz (1.2 kg) in size. Divide into portions, skin and pierce the flesh. Marinate overnight for best results. Cook in a very hot oven for about 20 minutes or under a very hot grill, turning two or three times, for about 15 minutes. Works well on a barbecue too.

Chicken Tikka

The majority of restaurants use thigh fillets for this dish but you might like to try breast meat for a change. Marinate for a minimum of 6 hours or overnight for even better flavor. This is great cooked on the barbecue. Or you might like to put the chunks of meat onto skewers and cook under a very hot grill for 10–15 minutes until cooked through.

Lamb Tikka and Lamb Chops

The meat for Lamb Tikka needs to be tender and lean. Use meat from the leg, or try lamb fillets. Trim the fat from the lamb chops. Marinate the meat overnight for best results.

Tandoori Beef or Pork

Marinate diced pork fillet or rump steak overnight. Place onto skewers and cook under a hot grill or over a barbecue.

Seafood

Fish and shrimp are delicious cooked in the tandoori way. Use fish with firm flesh and green (uncooked) shrimp if you can get them. Experiment with different varieties of fish such as trout or salmon; you really can't go wrong. Marinate seafood for 15–30 minutes only.

Paneer

Marinated and grilled cubes of paneer are delicious and nutritious if you prefer a vegetarian dish. Marinate for 2–3 hours, skewer and cook under a hot grill for a few minutes until crisp and golden. Alternate the pieces of paneer with marinated vegetables for a change.

Vegetables

Mushrooms are a good "meaty" vegetable and excellent done this way. Buy even-sized button mushrooms or the fuller-flavored field mushrooms. Wipe with a damp cloth (do not wash) and marinate for 3–4 hours. Baste with oil and cook under a very hot grill, turning once.

Serve your tandoori dishes sizzling (see page 42) with a sauce of your choice, a crisp green salad, and rice, naan bread or both.

10.   CHICKEN DISHES

M EAT AND poultry are not generally consumed daily in India, with some populations existing happily on a varied and nutritious diet consisting exclusively of grains, lentils, beans, vegetables and dairy foods. Chicken is a popular choice for nonvegetarian meals and is served in a myriad of tantalizing ways according to the style of cooking of the region or the styles adopted by restaurant chefs to create varied and tasty dishes for the restaurant menu.

Most of the curries served in Indian restaurants are made using chicken prepared and precooked every couple of days or so by the restaurant chef. Combined with a selection of spices, herbs and the curry sauce, they allow your meal to be served to you within minutes of you placing your order.

These preparation and cooking techniques, unique to restaurant cooking, also serve to differentiate the flavor and texture of Indian restaurant food from traditionally made dishes.

Using the method outlined here, you can precook the chicken, refrigerate or freeze it, and, together with some curry sauce, prepare one or more of the delicious curry recipes detailed in the following pages within about 20–25 minutes.

PREPARING CHICKEN

Preparation and cooking time: 25 minutes.
For 6–8 people you will require:

5 large chicken breast fillets, preferably free-range
    (approximately 2 lb/900 g with skin and bone removed)
6 tbsp olive oil
1 tsp turmeric
4 tbsp reserved curry sauce, prepared to the end of step 2
    (page 33)

With a sharp knife remove all fat and sinew from the chicken fillets, rinse and pat dry with paper towels. Cut each fillet into 8 equal-sized pieces, about 1 inch (2.5 cm) wide. Place the oil, turmeric and curry sauce into a large saucepan and mix well. Cook on medium heat, stirring continuously, until the sauce starts to darken in color (approximately 4–5 minutes).

Add the chicken and stir until all the pieces are well coated with the sauce. Turn down the heat, cover and continue cooking for 15–20 minutes, or until the chicken is tender, stirring frequently.

Remove the chicken pieces with a slotted spoon (leaving behind the remaining sauce) and place them in a clean container.

Use immediately or cool and refrigerate for up to 4 days.

Freezing: Freeze for up to 2 months.

TIP

If you don't have any reserved curry sauce, use 2 tablespoons of very finely chopped onion.

Chicken dishes

Chicken Methiwalla
Marinated chunks of chicken grilled and braised in a tasty, peppery, sun-dried fenugreek masala base.

Chicken Yogurt Curry
Tender pieces of chicken breast in a lightly tangy yogurt-based sauce, robustly spiced.

Mughlai Cashew Jhool
Mildly spiced, opulently rich with cashew-nut paste and finished with cream.

Chicken and Chickpea Curry
A satisfying combination of tender chicken breast, chickpeas and mushrooms in a mildly spiced coconut-milk sauce.

Chicken Chettinad
A stunning south Indian speciality with coconut and a fragrant blend of lightly roast spices, tomatoes and curry leaves.

Murgh Hariyali Masala
Tender breast pieces marinated in fresh herbs, green chilies and spices. A fresh and flavorsome dish.

Chicken Tikka Masala
The all-time favorite, marinated chunks of chicken grilled and braised in a creamy sauce.

Parsi Chicken with Apricots
Boneless chicken stir-fried in an aromatic spice blend and simmered in a thick sauce with fresh, fruity flavors.

Goan Coconut Chicken
Chicken pieces in a delicious, generously spiced, tamarind-flavored creamy coconut sauce.

CHICKEN METHIWALLA

Methi is the Indian name for fenugreek leaves, which have a distinctly aromatic "curryish" smell and flavor. This dish is inspired by northern India, where methi is used much like spinach in meat and vegetable curries and snacks. Unlike spinach, it adds a lot of delicious flavor.

Fenugreek leaves can be purchased in bunches, much like cilantro, from Indian markets and supermarkets and are also easily grown (see page 18). Sun-dried methi is available in small packs and is generally of good quality. It can be used in place of fresh leaves if these are not available, but fresh is definitely best.

SERVES 4	3 tbsp olive oil	1/2 tsp salt
Preparation and cooking time: 20–25 minutes	1 bunch (about 5 oz/150 g) fenugreek leaves, chopped (or 2 oz/50 g dried leaves) 15 fl oz (425 mL) curry sauce (page 32)	1/2 tsp chili powder 1 lb (450 g) precooked chicken fillets (page 59) 1 tsp garam masala

■ Heat the oil in a large, heavy-based frying pan and add the fenugreek leaves. If you are using fresh leaves, cook on low heat for about 10 minutes. If you are using dried leaves, stir in hot oil for a few seconds only.

■ Add the curry sauce, salt and chili powder and bring to a boil. Cook on high heat for about 5 minutes until the sauce is thick and the oil floats to the surface.

■ Add the chicken and bring to a boil. Stir in the garam masala and simmer for about 5 minutes, stirring frequently. Serve.

CHICKEN YOGURT CURRY

This is a lovely creamy dish but without the calories of cream, combining a modified version of an authentic Indian food (the yogurt curry) with tender morsels of chicken. For best results use fresh homemade yogurt (page 24) or buy the freshest, best-quality plain yogurt you can find. No curry sauce is required for this dish.

SERVES 4		
Preparation and cooking time: 30 minutes	9 fl oz (250 mL) plain yogurt 1 tbsp chickpea flour (besan) 1 tsp salt 7 fl oz (200 mL) cold water 2 tbsp olive oil 1 tsp black mustard seeds 1 tsp whole cumin seeds 1 onion, finely chopped 2 cloves of garlic	1-inch (2.5 cm) piece of ginger (or a portion of prepared garlic and ginger mix, page 30, thawed) 2 green chilies, finely chopped (or half a portion of prepared chilies, page 30) 1 tsp turmeric 1 lb (450 g) precooked chicken fillets (page 59) 1 tsp garam masala 1 tbsp finely chopped cilantro

■ In a large bowl, whisk together the yogurt, chickpea flour, salt and water. Heat the oil in a large, heavy-based saucepan, and add the mustard and cumin seeds. Fry for a few seconds on medium heat until they start to pop.

■ Add the onion and fry for about 5 minutes. Stir in the garlic, ginger and chilies and stir-fry for a couple of minutes longer.

■ Sprinkle on the turmeric, stir, and add the yogurt mixture. Bring to a boil stirring continuously and turn down the heat. Simmer, stirring frequently, for about 20 minutes.

■ Add the chicken and gently bring back to a simmer. Simmer for 5 minutes. Stir in the garam masala and cilantro. Serve.

MUGHLAI CASHEW JHOOL

Dishes thickened with rich nut pastes were first introduced to India by the Mughals who settled in the north of the country in 1525. The Mughal emperors brought with them opulence formerly unknown to the region. Money was no object to the extravagant settlers, and their imagination was boundless. Their favorite foods — almonds, cream and dried fruits — were lavishly incorporated into the traditional cuisine. This beautifully spiced, deliciously creamy dish reflects some of the grandeur of that bygone era.

SERVES 3–4

Preparation and cooking time: 20 minutes

3 tbsp olive oil
1/2 tsp ground cumin
1 tsp ground coriander
6 green cardamom pods, crushed
15 fl oz (425 mL) curry sauce (page 32)
1 tsp Kashmiri chili powder or 1/2 tsp chili powder and 1/2 tsp paprika

1 tsp salt
4 tbsp thick cream
2 oz (50 g) raw cashew nuts, processed until fine.
Note: Ground almonds may be used instead of cashews.
1 lb (450 g) precooked chicken fillets (page 59)

■ Heat the oil in a large, heavy-based frying pan and add the cumin, coriander and cardamom and fry for a few seconds. Add the curry sauce and bring to a boil.

■ Stir in the chili powder, paprika (if you are using it) and salt. Simmer for about 5 minutes and stir in the cream and ground nuts.

■ Simmer for another 5 minutes and stir in the chicken. Continue to cook on low heat for another 5 minutes, stirring often. Serve.

CHICKEN AND CHICKPEA CURRY

This delicious and unusual chicken curry is thought to originate on the southwest coast of India. It has distinct Goan and south Indian influences. The chickpeas and mushrooms make this curry almost a one-pot dish that is tasty, satisfying and nutritious.

SERVES 4–6

Preparation and cooking time: 30 minutes

3 tbsp olive oil
1 tsp black mustard seeds
2 cloves of garlic, sliced
1-inch (2.5 cm) piece of ginger, julienned
9 oz (250 g) mushrooms, sliced thickly
4 bay leaves, roughly torn
1-inch (2.5 cm) piece of cinnamon
4 cardamom pods, crushed
1 tsp ground coriander
1 tsp ground cumin

$1/2$ tsp chili powder
$1/2$ tsp turmeric
14 oz (400 g) can cooked chickpeas
15 fl oz (425 mL) curry sauce, page 32
$1/2$ tsp paprika
1 tsp salt
1 lb (450 g) precooked chicken fillets (page 59)
9 fl oz (250 mL) coconut milk
1 red chili, deseeded and sliced
1 tbsp chopped cilantro

■ Heat the oil in a deep, heavy-based frying pan and add the mustard seeds. Shake the pan over the heat for a few seconds until the seeds start to pop, and add the garlic, ginger and mushrooms.

■ Stir-fry for 3 minutes and add the bay leaves, cinnamon, cardamoms, coriander, cumin, chili and turmeric. Fry for a minute and stir in the chickpeas, curry sauce, paprika and salt.

■ Bring to a boil, and cook on high for 5 minutes until the sauce thickens. Add the chicken and coconut milk, bring back to a boil and simmer for 10 minutes.

■ Stir through the red chili and serve sprinkled with cilantro.

CHICKEN CHETTINAD

Chettinad, a prosperous region in Tamil Nadu, southern India, is renowned for its spice concoctions. Historically a trading region, spices were one of the main commodities traded. It is thought that this is why there is such an abundant use of spices in its cuisine. Therefore, this recipe does require a number of different spices, but once you smell the beautiful aroma of the roasted spices, I think you will feel it's worth it. Fresh coconut will produce the best results, but dried, shredded coconut is fine.

SERVES 4

Preparation and cooking time: 25–30 minutes

Spice mix
2 tsp olive oil
1 tsp poppy seeds
1/2 tsp fennel seeds
1/2 tsp coriander seeds
1/2 tsp black peppercorns
3–4 dried red chilies
just under 1-inch (2 cm) piece of cinnamon, broken into small pieces
5 green cardamom pods
2 cloves
1 tbsp grated coconut (or shredded coconut)

Remaining ingredients
2 tbsp olive oil
4 curry leaves
1 ripe tomato, chopped
15 fl oz (425 mL) curry sauce (page 32)
1/2 tsp salt
1/2 tsp chili powder
1 tsp paprika
1/2 tsp turmeric
1 lb (450 g) precooked chicken fillets (page 59)
4 cherry tomatoes, halved, or a large tomato sliced into 8 pieces
juice of half a lime
1 tbsp chopped cilantro

■ Heat the oil in a small pan and roast the spices and coconut on low heat for about a minute until aromatic. Cool and grind to a fine powder in a pestle and mortar or electric grinder.

■ Heat the remaining oil in a large, heavy-based frying pan and add the curry leaves, stir for a few seconds and add the chopped tomato. Stir-fry for 3 or 4 minutes until pulpy and add the spice mix. Fry on low heat for about 5 minutes, until the mixture starts releasing the oil.

■ Add the curry sauce, salt, chili powder, paprika and turmeric and bring to a boil. Simmer for about 5 minutes. The sauce will be quite thick because of the spice mix. Add a little water if required.

■ Add the chicken, bring back to a simmer and cook for 3 minutes. Stir in the tomatoes, lime juice and cilantro, and serve.

Murgh Hariyali Masala

This is absolutely delicious and so simple and quick to prepare. It is essential to use fresh herbs though; they are the backbone of this spectacular dish. Curry sauce is not required for this dish.

SERVES 3–4

Preparation and cooking time: 30 minutes (plus marinating time)

3 chicken fillets (about 1 lb or 450 g)
1 tsp salt
4 tbsp cilantro
4 tbsp mint leaves
4 fresh curry leaves
4 green garlic tops (optional)
4 spring onions
2–3 green chilies

1-inch (2.5 cm) piece of ginger, roughly chopped
2 cloves of garlic, roughly chopped
1 tsp garam masala
6 tbsp yogurt
2 tbsp olive oil
3 tbsp thick cream
1 tsp chickpea flour (besan)
3 fl oz (100 mL) hot water

■ Wash the chicken fillets, pat dry with paper towels, and cut into 1-inch (2.5 cm) chunks. Place in a large bowl.

■ Put the salt, herbs, spring onions, chilies, ginger, garlic, garam masala, yogurt and 1 tablespoon of the oil into the blender or food processor and process to a paste.

■ Add the herb paste to the chicken, mix well and refrigerate for 2–3 hours or overnight.

■ Remove from the fridge about half an hour before cooking and stir in the cream and chickpea flour.

■ Heat a wide, heavy-based (preferably nonstick) frying pan and add the remaining oil. Add the chicken and all the marinade to the pan and stir-fry on high heat until the chicken is opaque.

■ Turn down the heat a little, and continue to cook, stirring and turning the chicken pieces, until the sauce is quite dry, at which point it will release the oil (about 6–7 minutes).

■ Continue cooking for a few minutes longer until the chicken pieces start to brown slightly. Now add the water and stir in to create a thick, creamy sauce.

■ Simmer gently for 3 or 4 minutes. Add more water if you want a little more sauce.

■ Serve.

Note: The chickpea flour is important as it prevents the sauce from spitting.

CHICKEN TIKKA MASALA

No Indian restaurant cookbook could be complete without a recipe for the famous Chicken Tikka Masala.

Chicken Tikka Masala is probably, more than any other restaurant dish, a hybrid of Indian and Western tastes: *tikka* is a morsel of roasted meat, traditionally eaten without curry sauce or gravy, a practice seemingly unattractive to Western palates. The *masala* part of the dish is the Western touch that possibly came about in Glasgow in the 1960s when a long-suffering Indian chef mixed some spices and yogurt into canned tomato soup and presented his ever-complaining customers with the sauce they demanded. The rest, as they say, is history.

With a few enhancements since that fateful time, the dish has become an icon of Indian restaurant cuisine. Indeed, in 2001, Britain's foreign minister Robin Cook declared it to be Britain's "national dish" and the British consume vast amounts of it each week. It is, in fact, even more popular than fish and chips.

There are many recipes for Chicken Tikka Masala. This one is easy to prepare and quite delicious.

SERVES 3–4 **Preparation and cooking time:** **15 minutes**	4 tbsp olive oil 1/2 tsp ground cumin 15 fl oz (425 mL) curry sauce (page 32) 1 tsp paprika 1 tsp salt 1 level tsp chili powder	pinch of red food coloring (optional) 1 tsp garam masala 3 chicken fillets, freshly made into chicken tikka (page 58) 6 tbsp light cream 1 tbsp finely chopped cilantro

- Heat the oil in a large, deep frying pan, and stir in the cumin. Fry for a few seconds and add the curry sauce. Bring the sauce to a boil.

- Add the paprika, salt, chili powder and food coloring (if you are using it), and continue to cook on high heat, stirring frequently, for about 5 minutes or until the sauce thickens.

- Turn down the heat and stir in the garam masala. Simmer for about 3 minutes.

- Meanwhile, slice each piece of chicken tikka in two and add to the sauce. Stir in the cream and simmer for another 2–3 minutes.

- Serve sprinkled with the cilantro.

TIP

If you have a little Tandoori Marinade (page 57) left over, stir a couple of teaspoons of it into the sauce just before the cream. It adds extra color and flavor.

PARSI CHICKEN WITH APRICOTS

This delicious Parsi dish has a lovely balance of sweet and sour flavors derived from juicy apricots, soft brown sugar and vinegar. Lamb can be used instead of chicken for a change.

SERVES 4

Preparation and cooking time: 20–25 minutes

2 tbsp olive oil
2 tsp tomato paste
1/2 tsp turmeric
15 fl oz (425 mL) curry sauce (page 32)
1/2 tsp salt
1 tsp chili powder
1 tsp paprika

6 dried apricots, quartered
1 tsp soft brown sugar
1 tbsp vinegar
1 lb (450 g) precooked chicken fillets (page 59)
1 tbsp thick cream
1 tsp garam masala
1 tbsp chopped cilantro

■ Heat the oil in a large, heavy-based frying pan and add the tomato paste and turmeric. Stir-fry for a minute.

■ Add the curry sauce, salt, chili powder, paprika, apricots, sugar and vinegar. Bring to a boil and simmer for 5 minutes.

■ Stir in the chicken, bring back to a boil and simmer, stirring often, for 5 minutes.

■ Stir in the cream and garam masala. Simmer for a minute. Serve sprinkled with cilantro.

GOAN COCONUT CHICKEN

Nowhere is the Portuguese influence more evident than in the delicious and colorful cuisine of Goa. Although seafood and rice are the staples, this chicken recipe encompasses all that is good about Goan food. It has lots of tasty sauce to eat with rice and bread.

SERVES 4

Preparation and cooking time: 20–25 minutes

Spice mix
1/2 tsp fennel seeds
1/2 tsp fenugreek seeds
1/2 tsp black peppercorns
1 tsp coriander seeds
1 tsp cumin seeds
4 green cardamoms
4 cloves
1-inch (2.5 cm) piece of cinnamon

Remaining ingredients
3 tbsp olive oil
1/2 tsp turmeric
12 fl oz (325 mL) curry sauce (page 32)
1 tsp salt
1 tsp chili powder
1 tsp paprika
11 fl oz (300 mL) coconut cream
1 lb (450 g) precooked chicken fillets (page 59)
2 tsp tamarind paste dissolved in 2 tbsp warm water

■ Grind all the spices for the spice mix to a fine powder in a pestle and mortar or electric grinder.

■ Heat the oil in a large, heavy-based frying pan and add the spice mix. Fry on medium heat for about a minute until aromatic.

■ Stir in the turmeric, curry sauce, salt, chili powder and paprika. Bring to a boil and cook on high heat for about 3 minutes until thickened slightly. Turn down the heat.

■ Add the coconut cream and bring slowly to a simmer. Add the chicken to the sauce and mix well. Simmer for about 5 minutes.

■ Stir in the tamarind and serve.

11. LAMB DISHES

THROUGHOUT its long history, India has been invaded by foreign armies of traders and settlers from all over the world, beginning with the Greeks, led by Alexander the Great, as far back as 326 BCE, followed by many others from various destinations over the ages. The culinary influence of Greek, Middle Eastern, Portuguese and English invaders is clearly evident in Indian cuisine.

The rich and opulent Mughal settlers of the 16th century introduced meat dishes to the Indian nation, whose people had existed for centuries on grains, pulses, nuts, fruits and dairy products. Although goat is the preferred meat for the non-Muslim population, lamb is widely consumed throughout India.

Precooked lamb pieces are always in the restaurant fridge, ready to be combined with various herbs and spices according to the dish that is being prepared. Tender, good-quality meat is essential for most of the curries served in Indian restaurants, the tougher cuts being reserved for any traditional, slow-cooked dishes that may be on the menu.

Leg of lamb is the cut of choice for the majority of restaurant curries. Have a butcher remove the bone and trim the fat and gristle from the meat. Cut the remaining lean meat into 1-inch (2.5 cm) cubes and prepare as shown here. If you wish to use cuts with the bone in, increase the quantities accordingly.

Note: The meat has a tendency to dry out when refrigerated. Spoon some of the oil left in the pan onto the meat, coating each piece to keep it moist.

PREPARING LAMB

Serves 6–8

2 lb (900 g) boned, diced lamb
8 tbsp vegetable oil
1 tsp turmeric
4 tbsp reserved curry sauce, prepared to the end of step 2 (page 33)

Wash the meat and pat dry with paper towels. Place the oil, turmeric and curry sauce in a large saucepan and mix well. Cook on medium heat, stirring continuously until the sauce begins to darken in color (4–5 minutes).

Add the meat and stir until all the pieces are well coated. Turn down the heat and cook, covered, for 30–40 minutes or until the meat is tender. Add a little water to prevent the meat from sticking to the bottom of the pan and burning, and stir frequently.

Remove the lamb pieces using a slotted spoon, leaving behind the remaining sauce, and place in a clean container.

Use immediately, or cool and refrigerate for up to 4 days.

Freezing: Freeze for up to 2 months.

Lamb dishes

Parsi Lamb Curry
Boned, diced leg of lamb simmered in a tangy, aromatic spice mixture with garlic, ginger and tomatoes, served with crispy potato straws.

Lamb Kalia
Tender diced lamb and crisp potato chunks, in a lightly spiced sauce.

Bhindi Ghost
Lamb and okra curry. A fragrant mix of fresh okra, diced lamb and roasted spices in a tasty masala base.

Tamatar Ghost
Boneless diced lamb, braised with vine-ripened tomatoes, fresh herbs and spices.

Badami Lamb Pasanda
Marinated, tender strips of lamb fillet in a mildly spiced, lusciously creamy and aromatically flavorful sauce.

Kali Mirch Ka Ghost
Tender lamb pieces simmered in a spicy sauce flavored with gently roasted black peppercorns.

Mughal Lamb with Turnips
Succulent pieces of lamb, in a rich, dark sauce with sweet, juicy turnips. Inspired by the decadent Mughal era.

Rogan Josh
Tender pieces of lamb in a delicious thick sauce flavored with an aromatic spice blend. An old favorite.

PARSI LAMB CURRY

The unique fruity, spicy flavors of this dish are inspired by the Parsi style of cooking, which, in turn, is a combination of Gujerati and Iranian cuisine. The crispy fried potato straws, *sali*, add a lovely crunch to the dish.

SERVES 4		
Preparation and cooking time: 20–25 minutes	3 tbsp olive oil 1-inch (2.5 cm) stick of cinnamon 4 cardamom pods 6 curry leaves 1 tbsp tomato paste 15 fl oz (425 mL) curry sauce (page 32) 1 tbsp vinegar 2 tsp soft brown sugar	1 tsp chili powder $1/2$ tsp turmeric $1/2$ tsp salt 1 lb (450 g) precooked lamb (page 71) 1 tsp garam masala 1 tbsp chopped cilantro Sali, to serve (optional)

■ Heat the oil in a deep, heavy-based frying pan and add the cinnamon, cardamoms and curry leaves. Stir for a few seconds and add the tomato paste. Stir-fry for about a minute.

■ Stir in the curry sauce, vinegar, sugar, chili powder, turmeric and salt and bring to a boil. Cook the sauce on high heat for about 3 minutes until thickened slightly.

■ Add the lamb to the sauce and bring back to a boil. Stir in the garam masala and simmer gently for 5 minutes. Stir in the cilantro and ladle into a serving dish.

■ Sprinkle on the Sali (if it is being used) and serve.

SALI
(CRISPY POTATO STRAWS)

Grate or julienne 2 large peeled potatoes and soak in salted, chilled water for a few minutes.

Drain the potato well and spread on a tea towel until dry.

Deep-fry potato in hot oil until golden brown. Drain and serve with Parsi Lamb Curry.

Lamb Kalia

This dish of tender lamb and fried potatoes is based on the Kashmiri dish kalia. Kalia is traditionally made with mutton marinated in yogurt and ginger (to tenderize it), followed by long simmering, but the restaurant version is, by comparison, quick and easy to prepare. Sometimes fried cauliflower is also added to the dish with the potatoes.

SERVES 4

Preparation and cooking time: 25–30 minutes

2 medium-sized potatoes, peeled
1 tsp salt, plus a little extra
4 tbsp olive oil
1 onion, sliced
1-inch (2.5 cm) piece of ginger, grated
2 cloves of garlic, finely chopped
  (or a portion of prepared garlic-and-ginger
  mix, page 30, thawed)
7 fl oz (200 mL) plain yogurt

1 tsp chili powder
1/2 tsp paprika
1/2 tsp turmeric
1 tsp ground coriander
14 fl oz (400 mL) curry sauce (page 32)
1 lb (450 g) precooked lamb (page 71)
1/2 tsp garam masala
2 tbsp chopped cilantro

■ Cut the potatoes into approximately 1-inch (2.5 cm) chunks and cook in boiling, salted water for about 5 minutes or until just tender. Drain well and sprinkle lightly with a little salt.

■ While the potatoes are boiling, heat 1 tablespoon of the oil in a heavy-based frying pan and fry the onion slices until lightly browned. Set aside.

■ Combine the ginger, garlic, yogurt, chili powder, paprika, turmeric, salt and coriander in a small bowl.

■ Heat 2 tablespoons of the oil in the same pan used for the onions and add the yogurt mixture. Stir-fry for 3 minutes and add the curry sauce. Bring to a boil and simmer for 10 minutes until the sauce is thick and the oil rises to the surface.

■ Meanwhile, heat the remaining oil in another frying pan and fry the potato on medium heat, turning until all sides are golden.

■ Add the meat to the yogurt and curry sauce mixture and bring back to a boil. Add the garam masala and simmer for 5 minutes.

■ Stir half the potato chunks and half the cilantro into the onion mixture. Reheat for a minute. Serve sprinkled with the remaining crispy potato chunks and remaining cilantro.

BHINDI GHOST

The bhindi, also called okra or ladies' fingers, add an extra dimension to this dish by helping to thicken and flavor the sauce. Be careful not to cook the bhindi for more than the specified time as they have a tendency to become slimy. It is important to wash and dry the bhindi before slicing them for the same reason.

SERVES 4–5

Preparation and cooking time: 25–30 minutes

Spice mix
8 black peppercorns
3 cloves
1 tsp cumin seeds
1 tsp coriander seeds
4 green cardamom pods

Remaining ingredients
9 oz (250 g) bhindi (okra)
3 tbsp olive oil
1-inch (2.5 cm) piece of ginger, finely chopped
2 cloves of garlic, finely chopped
   (or a portion of prepared garlic-and-ginger
   mix, page 30, thawed)

2 green chilies, finely chopped (or half a portion
   of prepared chili, page 30)
2 ripe tomatoes, chopped
1 tsp salt
1 tsp turmeric
1/2 tsp chili powder
18 fl oz (525 mL) curry sauce (page 32)
1 lb (450 g) precooked lamb (page 71)
1/2 tsp garam masala
1 tbsp chopped cilantro

■   In a small dry pan, roast the peppercorns, cloves, cumin, coriander and cardamoms for about 2 minutes over medium heat. Remove the spices from the hot pan as soon as they become aromatic. Cool, and grind in a pestle and mortar or electric grinder.

■ Meanwhile, wash the bhindi whole, drain well and pat dry with paper towels or a clean tea towel until quite dry. Slice into 2-inch (5 cm) pieces.

■ Heat the oil in a deep, heavy-based frying pan and fry the ginger and garlic for about a minute. Add the green chilies and fry for another minute.

■ Stir in the tomatoes, salt and turmeric and cook over low heat for a few minutes until the tomatoes are soft and pulpy.

■ Add the bhindi to the pan, sprinkle the chili powder and roast spices onto the mixture. Stir-fry on medium heat for 4 or 5 minutes.

■ Add the curry sauce and bring to a boil, cook on medium heat for about 5 minutes, stirring frequently, until thickened.

■ Add the meat, bring back to a boil and simmer for another 5 minutes. Stir in the garam masala and cilantro, and serve.

Tamatar Ghost

Fresh ripe tomatoes add color, freshness and flavor to this simple lamb curry. High-quality, flavorful tomatoes are a must for a really tasty dish.

SERVES 4

Preparation and cooking time: 25–30 minutes

3 tbsp olive oil
1 tsp ground cumin
2 tsp ground coriander
2 ripe tomatoes, chopped
1/2 tsp salt
1/2 tsp turmeric
1/2 tsp chili powder

15 fl oz (425 mL) curry sauce (page 32)
1 lb (450 g) precooked lamb (page 71)
1/2 tsp garam masala
1/2 tsp dried ground fenugreek leaves
6 cherry tomatoes, halved
2 tbsp chopped cilantro

■ Heat the oil in a deep, heavy-based frying pan and add the cumin and coriander. Stir-fry for a few seconds and add the tomatoes, salt, turmeric and chili powder.

■ Stir-fry on high heat for a couple of minutes then turn down the heat and simmer the tomatoes on low heat, stirring frequently, until the mixture is pulpy, dark red and releasing the oil. This will take about 10 minutes.

■ Add the curry sauce and bring to a boil. Boil on high for about 5 minutes until the sauce has thickened.

■ Stir in the lamb and bring back to a boil. Add the garam masala and fenugreek leaves, and simmer for 5 minutes.

■ Stir through the cherry tomatoes and half the cilantro. Heat for about a minute.

■ Serve sprinkled with the remaining cilantro.

Badami Lamb Pasanda

Pasanda is a popular north Indian and Pakistani dish with its origins in the royal courts of the Mughal emperors. It is a deliciously fragrant and satisfying dish that is usually made with lamb but can be made with any meat, vegetable or with paneer. The lamb fillets used in this recipe cook really quickly and are beautifully tender, but leg meat works just as well with longer cooking.

SERVES 4

Preparation and cooking time: 30 minutes (plus marinating time of 15–30 minutes)

1 lb 2 oz (500 g) lamb fillets
2 cloves of garlic, minced or finely chopped
small piece of ginger, grated
  (or a portion of prepared garlic-and-ginger mix, page 30, thawed)
2 green chilies, finely chopped
  (or half a portion of prepared chili, page 30)
1 tbsp finely chopped mint leaves
3 tbsp plain yogurt
2 tbsp olive oil

1 tsp ground coriander
$1/2$ tsp ground cumin
$1/2$ tsp turmeric
15 fl oz (425 mL) curry sauce (page 32)
1 tsp salt
$1/2$ tsp paprika
4 tbsp half-and-half cream
1 tbsp ground almonds
$1/2$ tsp garam masala
1 tbsp rose water (optional)

■ Trim the lamb fillets, and using a meat mallet or rolling pin, flatten until just over $1/4$ inch (0.5 cm) thick. Cut into slices about $1 1/2$ inches (3.5 cm) long and just over $1/2$ inch (1 cm) wide.

■ Combine the garlic, ginger, chili, mint and yogurt in a medium bowl and add the meat. Stir well to coat the meat slices with the marinade. Leave to marinate for 15–30 minutes.

■ Heat the oil in a deep, heavy-based frying pan and carefully (it will splutter) add the meat and marinade. Stir-fry for about 3 minutes on medium-high heat or until most of the liquid evaporates.

■ Add the coriander, cumin and turmeric and stir-fry for a minute. Stir in the curry sauce and salt and bring to a boil. Turn down the heat and simmer for 10 minutes, stirring often, until the sauce thickens.

■ Stir in the paprika, cream and ground almonds and simmer for another 5 minutes, stirring regularly. Add the garam masala and heat through for a minute.

■ Remove from the heat and stir in the rose water, if you are using it. Serve.

KALI MIRCH KA GHOST

This dish of tender lamb pieces has a delicious peppery bite to it. Use whole black peppercorns, crushed, and don't be tempted to use ground black pepper.

SERVES 4

Preparation and cooking time: 15–20 minutes

1 tsp whole black peppercorns, crushed
3 tbsp olive oil
2 tsp ground coriander
1 tbsp tomato paste
1/2 tsp turmeric
15 fl oz (425 mL) curry sauce (page 32)

1/2 tsp salt
1 lb (450 g) precooked lamb (page 71)
4 whole green chilies, slit lengthwise
1/2 tsp garam masala
2 tbsp chopped cilantro

- Dry-roast the peppercorns in a small pan over medium heat for a minute or two until aromatic. Remove from the pan and set aside.

- Heat the oil in a deep, heavy-based frying pan and add the ground coriander. Stir-fry for a few seconds and stir in the tomato paste and turmeric.

- Cook on medium heat for 2 minutes and add the curry sauce and salt. Bring to a boil and cook on high heat, stirring often, until the sauce is really thick and the oil rises to the surface. This will take about 4–5 minutes.

- Add the lamb, roasted peppercorns and chilies. Bring back to a boil, stir in the garam masala and simmer gently, stirring often, for 5 minutes to allow the meat to absorb the flavors. Stir in half the cilantro.

- Serve sprinkled with the remaining cilantro.

MUGHAL LAMB WITH TURNIPS

The Mughals didn't do anything by halves and this dish is testament to that — this is a dish that in times of old would have been served in the royal palaces. Richly spiced, but not chili-hot, this is a dish to make when young, sweet turnips are in season.

If you can, use larger lamb pieces as prepared for Balti Meat (page 90) for more authenticity.

SERVES 4

Preparation and cooking time: 25–30 minutes

3 tbsp olive oil
2 tsp ground coriander
1 tsp ground cumin
3 green cardamom pods, crushed
1 tbsp tomato paste
1/2 tsp turmeric
2 green chilies, finely chopped (or a half portion of prepared chili, page 30)
9 oz (250 g) turnips, cut into chunks

15 fl oz (425 mL) curry sauce (page 32)
1 tsp paprika
1 tsp salt
1 lb 2 oz (500 g) precooked lamb (page 71) or prepared as for balti meat (page 90)
1/2 tsp garam masala
1 tbsp thick cream

■ Heat the oil in a deep, heavy-based frying pan and add the coriander, cumin and cardamom. Stir-fry for a few seconds and add the tomato paste, turmeric and green chilies.

■ Fry for 1 minute and stir in the turnips. Stir-fry on medium heat for 2 minutes and add the curry sauce, paprika and salt. Bring to a boil and simmer for 10 minutes.

■ Add the lamb and bring back to a boil and simmer again for 8–10 minutes or until the turnips are tender, the sauce has almost completely reduced and the oil has separated from the sauce.

■ Stir in the garam masala and cream, and cook for a minute longer. Serve.

Rogan Josh

Although there are many recipes available for Rogan Josh, it is such an old favorite I thought I would include it in this book as well. I have made some alterations to the classic recipe in keeping with changing tastes and demands.

SERVES 4		
Preparation and cooking time: 15–20 minutes	3 tbsp olive oil 1-inch (2.5 cm) stick of cinnamon 3 cloves 4 green cardamom pods 1 tsp ground coriander 1/2 tsp ground cumin 15 fl oz (425 mL) curry sauce (page 32)	2 tsp paprika 1 tsp chili powder 1/2 tsp salt 1 lb (450 g) precooked lamb (page 71) 1/2 tsp garam masala 4 tbsp plain yogurt 1 tbsp chopped cilantro

- Heat the oil in a deep, heavy-based frying pan and add the cinnamon stick, cloves, cardamoms, coriander and cumin. Stir-fry for a few seconds.

- Add the curry sauce, paprika, chili powder and salt, and bring to a boil. Continue to cook on high heat stirring often, for about 5 minutes or until the sauce has thickened.

- Add the meat and bring back to a boil. Turn down the heat and add the garam masala. Simmer for 5 minutes.

- Stir in the yogurt, 1 tablespoon at a time, waiting until each addition is completely incorporated before adding the next. Simmer and continue stirring for a minute after all the yogurt has been added.

- Serve sprinkled with the cilantro.

12. BALTI DISHES

SELL THE sizzle, not the steak? In the case of these dishes, it may be more accurate to say sell the sizzle *before* the steak.

First you hear the sizzle, and an instant later the delicious aroma arouses your senses and tickles your tastebuds as you wait in anticipation for the dish making its way to your table. And it does not disappoint. Generous quantities of succulent meats, tasty vegetables, fresh herbs and spices combined with thick flavorful sauces make these dishes quite memorable.

The origins of the balti dish can be traced back several centuries to a place called Baltistan, an area now located in the far north of Pakistan. It was introduced to England in the 1960s with the opening of the first "balti house" in Birmingham. The freshly cooked, wonderfully aromatic, gently spiced curries were such a hit with the British that within a few years hundreds of balti houses sprung up all over the UK. Balti refers to the people of Baltistan, the origins of the dish and the woklike utensil in which it is served.

The Indian *balti* (utensil), also known as *karahi*, and the Chinese wok are very much the same in shape and structure, though which came first is impossible to determine. China had long had an association with India through its trading routes with the inevitable influences on the two ancient cultures and their cuisines. The influence of the spicy dishes of Szechuan is subtly evident in the balti curry.

In terms of Indian restaurant cooking, the balti and karahi essentially started life as the same thing, though the dishes they now represent have evolved to take on slightly differing characteristics. The balti dishes retain their original concept and favor more subtle combinations and flavors while the karahi dishes have been designed to deliver a more authentic taste with stronger spice and herb mixes.

To get the sizzle that is synonymous with these dishes, heat your balti or karahi until very hot and carefully (it will splutter and splash) transfer the simmering curry into it. Serve immediately.

BALTI CURRIES

BALTI CHICKEN
A sumptuous dish with succulent chicken pieces, stir-fried with whole spices, tomatoes, sweet peppers and onions, served sizzling.

BALTI FISH
Fish pieces, served in the balti style, subtly spiced in a delicious creamy sauce.

BALTI SUBZI
A delicious combination of cauliflower, carrots, sweet peppers, potatoes and fresh cilantro.

BALTI MEAT
Tender pieces of lamb, beef or goat meat in a thick, tasty sauce with spices, sweet peppers, onions and tomatoes.

BALTI CHICKEN

This is a popular dish dating back to the original balti houses in Birmingham. I have used chicken breast fillets in this recipe, but you can use chicken portions on the bone if you wish for a more traditional dish. Allow an extra 15 minutes or so cooking time for chicken on the bone.

SERVES 4	3–4 chicken fillets (about 1 lb 2 oz or 500 g)	15 fl oz (425 mL) curry sauce (page 32)
	4 tbsp olive oil	1 tsp salt
Preparation and cooking time: 30 minutes	2–3 green garlic tops, chopped (optional)	1/2 tsp chili powder
	1/2 tsp cumin seeds	1/2 tsp paprika
	1/2 tsp ground cumin	1 medium-sized onion
	1 tsp ground coriander	1 green pepper
	1-inch (2.5 cm) stick of cinnamon	1 tomato
	4 green cardamoms	1/2 tsp garam masala
	1/2 tsp turmeric	1 tbsp chopped cilantro

■ Wash the chicken fillets and pat dry with paper towels. Trim off fat and sinew and slice each fillet into 4 pieces.

■ Heat 3 tablespoons of the oil in a large, deep frying pan, add the chopped garlic tops (if you are using them) and stir-fry for 3 or 4 minutes.

■ Add the cumin, coriander, cinnamon, cardamoms and turmeric. Stir for a few seconds until aromatic and add the chicken pieces.

■ Stir-fry the chicken for about 5 minutes on medium to high heat and add the curry sauce, salt, chili powder and paprika. Bring to a boil, stir and turn down the heat. Leave to simmer for about 15 minutes, stirring now and then.

■ Meanwhile, peel and quarter the onion. Slice each quarter into two. Slice the green pepper in half and deseed. Cut into approximately 1-inch (2.5 cm) squares. Quarter the tomato.

■ Heat the remaining oil in a clean pan and add the onion and green pepper. Stir-fry on high heat for 3 or 4 minutes until the onion just starts to color at the edges. Add the tomato and stir.

■ Add the onion, green pepper and tomato to the chicken and sprinkle on the garam masala. Continue to simmer for another 5 minutes or so, by which time the sauce should be thick and the oil should be separating from the sauce.

■ While the chicken is simmering, heat balti dishes on medium heat for about a minute. Carefully spoon the hot curry into the dishes, sprinkle on the cilantro and serve.

Balti Fish

Use any firm fish, including salmon if you like. Jumbo shrimp are fantastic for this dish, or try a combination of seafood.

SERVES 4	1 lb 2 oz (500 g) fish fillets or jumbo shrimp	1 tsp salt
Preparation and cooking time: 20–25 minutes	3 tbsp olive oil	1/2 tsp paprika
	1/2 tsp turmeric	1 medium-sized onion
	1/2 tsp chili powder	1 green pepper
	2 spring onions, chopped	1 tomato
	1/2 tsp ground cumin	1/2 tsp garam masala
	1/2 tsp ground coriander	juice of half a lemon
	15 fl oz (425 mL) curry sauce (page 32)	1 tbsp chopped cilantro

■ Wash the fish fillets or shrimp (shell and devein if you are using whole shrimp). Pat dry with paper towels. Cut the fish into large chunks about 2 inches (5 cm) in size.

■ Place the fish with about a tablespoon of the oil in a bowl. Sprinkle on a little of the turmeric and chili powder, and cover while preparing the sauce.

■ Heat 1 tablespoon of the oil in a large, deep frying pan, add the spring onions and stir-fry for 2 minutes.

■ Add the cumin, coriander and remaining turmeric. Stir for a few seconds until aromatic and add the curry sauce, salt, remaining chili powder and paprika. Bring to a boil, stir and turn down the heat. Leave the sauce to simmer and reduce for about 10 minutes, stirring now and then.

■ Meanwhile, peel and quarter the onion. Slice each quarter into two. Slice the green pepper in half and deseed. Cut into approximately 1-inch (2.5 cm) squares. Quarter the tomato.

■ Heat the remaining oil in a clean pan and add the onion and green pepper. Stir-fry on high heat for 3 or 4 minutes until the onion just starts to color at the edges. Add the tomato and stir.

■ Stir the onion, green pepper and tomato into the sauce with the garam masala. Simmer.

■ Wipe clean and heat the pan used to fry the vegetables. Add the fish chunks or shrimp to the pan and cook on medium to high heat until beginning to color. Sprinkle on the lemon juice.

■ Add the fish to the sauce and vegetables and stir through carefully to avoid breaking the fish pieces. Simmer until the fish is cooked through, about 5 minutes. Fish will flake easily when it is cooked, shrimp will be opaque.

■ Meanwhile heat balti dishes on medium heat for about a minute. Carefully spoon the curry into the dishes, sprinkle on the cilantro and serve with rice and breads.

Balti Subzi

This recipe uses a combination of cauliflower, carrots, sweet peppers and potatoes but you can use a combination of peas, mushrooms, green beans, eggplant, cabbage or any other vegetables that are in season and at their best.

SERVES 4–6

Preparation and cooking time: 30–35 minutes

approx. 8 oz (225 g) fresh cauliflower florets
1 large potato, peeled and cut into large chunks
2 carrots, peeled and diced
4 tbsp olive oil
2 spring onions, chopped
2–3 green garlic tops (optional)
1 small green pepper, deseeded and cut into squares
1 small red pepper, deseeded and cut into squares
1/2 tsp ground cumin

1/2 tsp ground coriander
1/2 tsp turmeric
2 ripe tomatoes, cut into small dice
11 fl oz (300 mL) curry sauce (page 32)
1 tsp salt
1/2 tsp chili powder
1/2 tsp garam masala
2 tbsp chopped cilantro

■ Boil or steam the cauliflower, potato and carrots until almost tender.

■ Meanwhile, heat the oil in a large, deep frying pan, add the spring onions and garlic tops (if you are using them), and stir-fry for 2 or 3 minutes. Add the red and green peppers and stir-fry for another 2 or 3 minutes.

■ Stir in the cumin, coriander and turmeric. Stir for a few seconds until aromatic and add the tomatoes. Stir-fry for a minute or two until the tomatoes are pulpy. Stir in the precooked cauliflower, carrots and potato.

■ Add the curry sauce to the vegetables with the salt and chili powder. Bring to a boil.

■ Turn down the heat and simmer the vegetables on low heat for about 15 minutes until the liquid has almost evaporated. There should just be a thick sauce clinging to the vegetables.

■ Stir the garam masala and half the fresh cilantro into the curry.

■ Heat balti dishes on medium heat for about a minute. Carefully spoon the curry into the dishes, sprinkle on the remaining cilantro and serve.

BALTI MEAT

Traditionally, the fresh goat, beef or lamb used for balti curries would be simmered over low fires for several hours. Obviously this is not practical for restaurant cuisine, and apart from chicken fillets and fish, which cook in minutes, the meat for the balti dish below needs to be preprepared to the stage where, with the addition of a few spices and fresh herbs, you can have a delicious and authentic balti curry ready in minutes. Prepare the meat as indicated for lamb curries (page 71), but cut it into larger chunks.

You can use any meat of your choice. Lamb is the preferred meat in most Indian restaurants, but the dish works just as well with beef.

SERVES 4

Preparation and cooking time: 20–25 minutes

4 tbsp olive oil
2–3 green garlic tops, chopped (optional)
1/2 tsp ground cumin
1 tsp ground coriander
1/2 tsp turmeric
1 lb 2 oz (500 g) lamb or other meat prepared as on page 71
18 fl oz/1 US pint (500 mL) curry sauce (page 32)

1 tsp salt
1/2 tsp chili powder
1/2 tsp paprika
1 medium-sized onion
1 green pepper
1 tomato
1/2 tsp garam masala
1 tbsp chopped cilantro

■ Heat 1 tablespoon of the oil in a large, deep frying pan, add the chopped garlic tops (if you are using them) and stir-fry for 3 or 4 minutes. Add the cumin, coriander and turmeric. Stir for a few seconds until aromatic and add the cooked meat.

■ Stir-fry for a minute or so and add the curry sauce, salt, chili powder and paprika. Bring to a boil, stir and turn down the heat. Leave to simmer for about 15 minutes, stirring now and then.

■ Meanwhile, peel and quarter the onion. Slice each quarter into two. Slice the green pepper in half and deseed. Cut into approximately 1-inch (2.5 cm) squares. Quarter the tomato.

■ Heat the remaining oil in a clean pan and add the onion and green pepper. Stir-fry on high heat for 3 or 4 minutes until the onion just starts to color at the edges. Add the tomato and stir.

■ Add the onion, green pepper and tomato to the meat and sprinkle on the garam masala. Continue to simmer for another 5 minutes or so, by which time the sauce should be thick and the oil should be separating from the sauce.

■ While the meat is simmering, heat balti dishes on medium heat for about a minute. Carefully spoon the hot curry into the dishes, sprinkle on the cilantro and serve.

13.

KARAHI AND OTHER TRADITIONAL DISHES

Popular restaurant dishes like chicken tikka masala evolved from modifications of traditional dishes adapted to be gentler on unsuspecting Western tastebuds. As the Western palate has become accustomed to Indian cuisine, tastes have changed and there is now a significant demand for more pungent flavors. To satisfy this demand, Indian restaurants are serving more authentic dishes. This chapter shows you how to make some of the most popular of these dishes with the same ease and convenience as the other restaurant curries.

KAHARI DISHES

The Indian *karahi* is the same utensil as the *balti*; however, the karahi curries served in Indian restaurants are spicier adaptations of the traditional balti dishes. These and the other traditional dishes in this section are wonderful if you are a curry fanatic who loves the robust flavor of Indian spice and herb combinations.

Karahi curries

Karahi Subzi
A mix of fresh seasonal vegetables in a dry, spicy and aromatic sauce.

Karahi Chicken
Pieces of chicken on the bone cooked with ginger, garlic and chilies in a thick, spicy sauce, served sizzling.

Karahi Keema
Minced lamb richly flavored with ginger, garlic and chilies.

Karahi Meat
Generous pieces of lamb on the bone in a rich, pungently aromatic and spicy sauce.

KARAHI SUBZI

You can use whatever vegetables are in season for this dish. I have used eggplants cooked with onions. This delicious recipe is generous with the oil as eggplants soak it up, making them lovely and silky.

SERVES 4–6		

Preparation and cooking time: 30 minutes	6 small long eggplants (approx. 12 oz or 350 g)
	6 tbsp of olive oil
	2 cloves of garlic, finely chopped
	1-inch (2.5 cm) piece of ginger, finely chopped
	  (or a portion of prepared garlic-and-ginger
	  mix, page 30, thawed)
	3 green chilies, finely sliced (or a portion of
	  prepared chili, page 30)
	2 large onions, sliced
	6 spring onions, white part only
		1 tsp fennel seeds
		1 tsp cumin seeds
		1 tsp fenugreek seeds
		1 tsp onion seeds
		1 tsp turmeric
		1 tsp chili powder
		2 tsp salt
		5 fl oz (150 mL) curry sauce (page 32)
		6 cherry tomatoes (optional)
		1 tsp garam masala

■ Wash and wipe the eggplants. Slice in half and cut each half into 2 slices.

■ Heat the oil in a karahi or large, heavy-based frying pan and add the garlic, ginger and chilies. Fry for a minute.

■ Add the eggplant and both types of onion to the pan and stir-fry on high heat until the vegetables begin to brown, about 5 minutes.

■ Pull the vegetables towards the edges of the pan and let the oil pool in the middle. Place all the seeds into the hot oil and stir them around for a minute or two on medium heat, and then stir them into the vegetables.

■ Sprinkle the turmeric, chili powder and salt on top, and cook for a minute longer before stirring in the curry sauce.

■ Bring to a boil, turn down the heat and simmer for about 5 minutes, stirring now and then. Add the tomatoes if you are using them and simmer for another 5 minutes. Stir through the garam masala and cook for a minute more.

■ Meanwhile, heat karahi dishes for about a minute on medium to high heat. Carefully transfer the curry to the hot karahis and serve sizzling.

Karahi Chicken

Traditionally, the bone is left in providing extra flavor and richness to the sauce, but chicken fillets can be used instead. You can also use the chicken prepared as for chicken curries (page 59) to speed up the preparation, but, if you have time, it is worth trying this dish the traditional way.

SERVES 6–8

Preparation and cooking time:
Step 1:
45 minutes
(30 minutes if using fillets)

Step 1: Preparing the chicken
1 chicken approx. 4 lb (1.8 kg), preferably free-range
2 tbsp olive oil
1 red onion, finely sliced
2 cloves of garlic, ground to a paste
1-inch (2.5 cm) piece of ginger, ground to a paste (or a portion of prepared garlic-and-ginger mix, page 30, thawed)

2 green chilies, finely chopped (or a portion of prepared chilies, page 30)
2 tsp salt
2 ripe tomatoes, chopped

- Have a butcher skin the chicken, separate the wings and drumsticks and chop the rest of the chicken into 8 pieces. Rinse the chicken portions well and drain.

- Heat the oil in a large, heavy-based saucepan and add the onion. Stir around for a minute or two and add the garlic, ginger and chilies. Stir-fry for 2 or 3 minutes until aromatic.

- Add the chicken and stir to coat in the oil, then add the salt and tomatoes. Stir-fry until sizzling. Stir in 2 tablespoons of water.

- Turn down the heat and simmer, covered, for about 30 minutes (10–15 minutes if you are using sliced chicken fillets), stirring occasionally until the chicken is just cooked through and most of the liquid has evaporated.

- Use immediately or cool and refrigerate or freeze for later use.

Preparation and cooking time: Step 2: 20–25 minutes	**Step 2: Preparing the curry** 2 tbsp olive oil 1 tsp turmeric 2 tsp garam masala	1–2 tsp chili powder to taste 18 fl oz/1 US pint (500 mL) curry sauce (page 32) 2 tbsp chopped cilantro

■ Heat the oil in a large, heavy-based frying pan or saucepan, and add the turmeric, half the garam masala and the chili powder. Cook, while stirring, for a minute or so until aromatic.

■ Add the cooked chicken and juices and stir to coat in the spices. Once it is bubbling, turn down the heat and simmer, covered, for about 10 minutes, stirring frequently to allow the chicken to absorb the flavors. There should be very little liquid at this stage so that everything is gently frying in the oil.

■ Add the curry sauce and bring back to a boil. Turn down the heat and simmer for another 8–10 minutes until the sauce is thick and the oil has separated from the sauce. Stir in the remaining garam masala and half the cilantro.

■ Meanwhile, heat karahi dishes for about a minute on medium heat, carefully pour in the curry, sprinkle with the remaining cilantro and serve.

Karahi Keema

Similar to Keema Peas but spicier, this is a delicious dish eaten with chapatis, spiced yogurt and pickles (*achar*).

SERVES 4–5

Preparation and cooking time:
Step 1:
45 minutes

Step 1: Preparing the meat
2 tbsp olive oil
2 red onions, sliced
1 lb 2 oz (500 g) lean minced lamb

1$\frac{1}{2}$ tsp salt
1 tsp turmeric
1 can (14 oz or 400 g) of chopped tomatoes

■ Heat the oil in a large, heavy-based saucepan, and add the onions. Stir around for 2 or 3 minutes over high heat and add the meat.

■ Stir-fry the meat and onions over high heat, breaking up any lumps, until the meat changes color, about 3 or 4 minutes. Turn down the heat, stir in the salt, turmeric and tomatoes.

■ Bring to a boil and turn down the heat. Simmer, uncovered, over low heat for about 30–35 minutes, stirring now and then, until all the liquid has evaporated.

■ Use immediately or cool and refrigerate or freeze for later use.

| Preparation and cooking time:
Step 2:
15–20 minutes | **Step 2: Preparing the curry**
2 tbsp olive oil
6 curry leaves (optional)
4 cloves of garlic, ground to a paste
1-inch (2.5 cm) piece of ginger, ground to a paste
  (or a portion of prepared garlic-and-ginger mix,
  page 30, thawed)
2 tsp julienned ginger (optional) | 2 green chilies, finely chopped (or half a portion of
  prepared chilies, page 30, thawed)
1 tsp ground cumin
1 tsp paprika
1 tsp chili powder
9 fl oz (250 mL) curry sauce (page 32)
7 oz (200 g) frozen peas
1 tsp garam masala |

■   Heat the oil in a large, heavy-based frying pan and add the curry leaves (if you are using them), and fry for a few seconds.

■   Add the garlic, ginger, chilies and cumin, and stir-fry for a couple of minutes until aromatic. Stir in the paprika and chili powder.

■   Add the meat to the pan and stir-fry until sizzling. Stir in the curry sauce and bring to a boil. Add the peas and bring to a boil again.

■   Turn down the heat and simmer for 10–15 minutes until quite dry. Stir in the garam masala and cook for a minute to allow the meat to absorb the spices.

■   Meanwhile heat karahi dishes for a minute on medium to high heat and carefully ladle in the meat. Serve.

KARAHI MEAT

Shoulder of lamb is superb for this recipe because it lends itself to long, slow cooking after which the meat is deliciously spiced and tender and almost falling off the bone. You can use leg of lamb cut into 2-inch (5 cm) chunks if you prefer.

SERVES 4–6

Preparation and cooking time:
Step 1:
2–2½ hours

Step 1: Preparing the meat
2 lb 4 oz (1 kg) lamb shoulder, cut into large pieces
2 tbsp olive oil
2 red onions, finely sliced
2 cloves of garlic, ground to a paste
1-inch (2.5 cm) piece of ginger, ground to a paste
   (or a portion of prepared garlic-and-ginger mix, page 30, thawed)

2 green chilies, finely chopped (or a portion of prepared chilies, page 30)
2 tsp salt
2 ripe tomatoes, chopped

■ Rinse the meat, drain well and pat dry with paper towels (wet meat will not brown).

■ Heat the oil in a large, heavy-based saucepan and add the onions. Stir around for a minute or two on high heat and add the lamb pieces. Stir around in the hot oil until the meat colors, about 5 minutes.

■ Add the garlic, ginger and chilies to the meat, stir-fry for a minute or two and add the salt. Stir and turn down the heat. Cook covered, stirring occasionally, for 1 hour.

■ Stir in the tomatoes and cook for another 45 minutes to an hour until the meat is tender and a rich, dark brown.

■ Skim off any excess fat and either use immediately, or cool and refrigerate or freeze for later use.

Preparation and cooking time: Step 2: 30 minutes	**Step 2: Preparing the curry** 2 tbsp olive oil 1 tsp ground cumin 2 tsp turmeric 2 tsp garam masala	1–2 tsp chili powder to taste 1 tbsp tomato paste 1 tsp dried ground fenugreek leaves 18 fl oz (500 mL) curry sauce (page 32) 2 tbsp chopped cilantro

■ Heat the oil in a large, heavy-based frying pan or saucepan, and add the cumin, turmeric, half the garam masala, chili powder and tomato paste.

■ Cook, stirring, for a few seconds, then add the cooked meat and juices and stir to coat in the spices.

■ Once it is bubbling, turn down the heat and simmer, covered, for about 10 minutes, stirring now and then to allow the meat to absorb the flavors. There should be very little liquid so that everything is gently frying in an oily masala. Sprinkle on the fenugreek leaves.

■ Add the curry sauce and bring back to a boil. Turn down the heat and simmer for 8–10 minutes until the sauce is thick and the oil begins to separate from it.

■ Stir in the remaining garam masala and half the cilantro.

■ Meanwhile, heat karahi dishes for about a minute on medium to high heat, carefully pour in the curry, sprinkle with the remaining cilantro and serve.

Other traditional dishes

Dhal Makhani
A deliciously earthy, creamy dhal of mixed lentils and pulses flavored with ginger, garlic and onions.

Chicken Jhol
Chicken pieces cooked with a traditional mix of onions, garlic and ginger and spiced with mustard seeds, cloves, cinnamon and pepper, and a touch of vinegar.

Dhesi Chicken
Punjabi fare with succulent pieces of chicken, onions, ginger, garlic, chilies and fresh herbs. A superb balance of authentic tastes in a delicious sauce.

Dhesi-style Saag
A traditional dish, this is a mix of greens, simmered until tender, pureed and flavored with ginger, garlic and chilies.

Dhaba-style Lamb Curry
Lamb Punjabi style. Boneless lamb in a rich, thick sauce flavored with lamb bones, onions, ginger, garlic, green chilies and fresh herbs.

Yogurt Curry
A tangy, hot and flavorsome mix of potatoes, onions, whole spices and fresh and dried herbs simmered in a yogurt sauce thickened with chickpea flour.

Achari Ghost
Lamb simmered in pickling spices — fennel, onion and mustard seeds; a dish with delicious and robust flavors.

Punjabi Cabbage
From the rich terrain of northern India, freshly sliced cabbage stir-fried with whole cumin, ginger and spices.

Shikari Ghost
Lamb with the bone in, cooked in the traditional way of the Indian hunters.

DHAL MAKHANI

For something so simple, this is quite a sumptuous dish — thick, creamy and satisfying. You can use 100 percent urad dhal or a mix of dhals (pulses) as I have. Traditionally made with generous amounts of ghee and homemade butter (*makhan*), this recipe uses olive oil and a little cream.

SERVES 4–6

Preparation and cooking time: 2 hours (or 30 minutes if you are using a pressure cooker)

5 oz (150g) urad dhal (black gram)
2 oz (50 g) moong dhal (mung bean)
2 oz (50 g) yellow split chana
35 fl oz/2.1 US pints (1 L) cold water
4 tbsp olive oil
1 small onion, finely chopped
2 cloves of garlic, finely chopped
1-inch (2.5 cm) piece of ginger, finely chopped
    (or a portion of prepared garlic-and-ginger mix,
    page 30, thawed)

2 green chilies, finely chopped (or half a portion of
    prepared chilies, page 30)
1 tsp dried ground fenugreek leaves (optional)
2 tsp salt
1 tsp garam masala
1 tbsp chopped cilantro
2 tbsp thick cream

■ Mix all three dhals in a bowl and wash well. Drain and place the dhals in a large, heavy-based saucepan and add the water.

■ Bring to a boil, turn down the heat and cover the pan. Simmer gently for about 2 hours, stirring now and then, until the mixture is thick and creamy, adding a little more water if required. Or bring the pressure cooker to maximum pressure and cook for about 25 minutes.

Note: The dhal can be cooled and refrigerated at this stage for later use. It will keep well in the fridge for up to 3 days.

■ Meanwhile, heat the oil in a frying pan or small saucepan and fry the onion until beginning to brown at the edges.

■ Add the garlic, ginger and chilies and fry for a couple of minutes until aromatic. Stir in the fenugreek leaves if you are using them.

■ Add the onion mixture, salt, garam masala and cilantro to the dhal and mix well. Simmer for a minute.

■ Stir in the cream and serve.

CHICKEN JHOL

This is a delicious chicken curry with robust flavors. It is typical of the flavors of eastern India. For those who have savored its delicious taste, it invokes memories such as this, as shared on the Indian cuisine blog, *Hesel Ghor*:

> Remember those hurried meals put together at the end of a hard day's travel at dimly lit circuit houses or government dak-bungalows. Thrown together by the chowkidar-caretaker-cook, the taste still lingers on. Probably the wonder of childhood, when things were so much more mysterious and the whole world was waiting to be discovered was the magic of the dish.

SERVES 3–4

Preparation and cooking time: 30–35 minutes

3 chicken fillets (about 1 lb or 450 g)
3 tbsp olive oil
2-inch (5 cm) stick of cinnamon
1 tsp black peppercorns
6 cardamoms
6 cloves
1 tsp black mustard seeds
2 tsp ground coriander
1 tsp ground cumin
2 cloves of garlic, finely chopped

1-inch (2.5 cm) piece of ginger, finely chopped
(or a portion of prepared garlic-and-ginger mix, page 30, thawed)
1/2 tsp turmeric
1 tsp tomato paste
2 tsp vinegar
15 fl oz (425 mL) curry sauce (page 32)
1 tsp salt
1–2 tsp chili powder
1 tbsp chopped cilantro

- Rinse the chicken fillets and pat dry with paper towels. Trim off fat and sinew and slice each fillet into 1-inch (2.5 cm) chunks.

- Heat the oil in a large, deep frying pan, add the cinnamon, peppercorns, cardamoms, cloves, mustard seeds, coriander and cumin, and stir-fry for a few seconds until the seeds start to pop.

- Add the garlic and ginger, and fry for about a minute until aromatic. Stir in the turmeric, tomato paste and vinegar.

- Add the chicken pieces and mix well to coat with the spices. Stir-fry the chicken on medium-high heat for about 5 minutes.

- Add the curry sauce, salt and chili powder, and bring to a boil. Turn down the heat and simmer for about 15–20 minutes until the chicken is tender and the sauce is thick.

- Stir in the chopped cilantro and serve.

DHESI CHICKEN

This is a beautiful, full-flavored dish with big, tender pieces of chicken on the bone and lots of lovely sauce. Traditionally it was made with older, tougher birds that required long, slow cooking, which enhanced the flavor as well as tenderizing the meat. I recommend using good-quality free-range chicken and fresh herbs to experience the best of this dish.

SERVES 4–6

Preparation and cooking time: 40–45 minutes with preprepared meat

3 tbsp olive oil
6 spring onions, chopped
6 green garlic tops, chopped (optional)
3 oz (100 g) fenugreek leaves, chopped (or 1 tsp dried ground fenugreek)
2 cloves of garlic, ground to a paste
1-inch (2.5 cm) piece of ginger, ground to a paste (or a portion of prepared garlic-and-ginger mix, page 30, thawed)
3–4 green chilies, finely chopped (or a portion of prepared chilies, page 30, thawed)

1 tsp turmeric
2 tsp garam masala
1 tsp chili powder
1 chicken approx. 4 lb (1.8 kg), prepared and cooked as for Karahi Chicken (page 94)
2 potatoes, peeled and cut into large chunks
18 fl oz/1 US pint (500 mL) curry sauce (page 32)
9 fl oz (250 mL) boiling water
2 tbsp chopped cilantro

- Heat the oil in a large, heavy-based saucepan and add the spring onions and garlic tops, if you are using them. Stir-fry on medium heat for 4–5 minutes. Add the fenugreek leaves and continue to stir-fry for 5 minutes.

- Add the garlic, ginger and chilies. Stir-fry on medium heat for 2 or 3 minutes and add the turmeric, half the garam masala and the chili powder. Cook, while stirring, for a minute or so until aromatic.

- Add the cooked chicken, including the juices, and stir to coat in the spices. Once it is bubbling, turn down the heat and simmer, covered, for about 10 minutes, stirring frequently to allow the chicken to absorb the flavors.

- Meanwhile, boil the potatoes in salted water for 8–10 minutes until just tender. Drain.

- Add the curry sauce to the chicken and bring back to a boil. Stir in the cooked potato, turn down the heat and simmer for another 8–10 minutes, stirring now and then, until the sauce is thick and the oil has separated from the sauce.

- Add the water and simmer for 2 minutes. Stir in the remaining garam masala and the cilantro, and serve.

DHESI-STYLE SAAG

Paneer, lamb, chicken and potato dishes made with pureed spinach (*saag*) are popular in Indian restaurants, but saag is rarely if ever served on its own. The tinned, pureed spinach used in restaurants is convenient and quite good when incorporated into other flavorful ingredients, but it does not compare with the saag made with fresh, leafy greens that is cooked in Indian households and eaten as a dish in its own right with cornmeal chapatis (rotis), yogurt and pickles. Meat and vegetarian dishes made with this saag are superb.

It is time consuming to make but you can cook a large batch and freeze it in serving-size portions that will be ready to use whenever you wish. You will need a large saucepan for this.

SERVES 8–10	
Preparation and cooking time: 3 hours 30 minutes (or 1 hour 30 minutes if you are using a pressure cooker)	14 oz (400 g) spring greens, mustard greens or purple sprouting broccoli 1 bunch of spinach (approx. 14 oz or 400 g) 9 oz (250 g) brussels sprouts 1 large head of broccoli (approx. 11 oz or 300 g) approx. 40 fl oz/3.2 US pints (1.5 L) cold water 3 tsp salt

4 cloves of garlic, ground to a paste (or a portion of prepared garlic-and-ginger mix, page 30, thawed)
2-inch (5 cm) piece of ginger, ground to a paste
2–3 green chilies, finely chopped (or a portion of prepared chilies, page 30)
5 oz (150 g) cornmeal (fine polenta)

- Wash the greens and spinach two or three times in plenty of cold water to remove all grit and soil, then drain. Remove any tough stalks from the spinach. Remove the outer leaves of the brussels sprouts and rinse well. Rinse the broccoli.

- Shred the greens and spinach, roughly chop the sprouts and broccoli, or process in a food processor until roughly chopped, and place in a saucepan.

- Add the water and salt, and bring to a boil. If you are using a pressure cooker, cook on maximum pressure for 45 minutes. Otherwise simmer, uncovered, for about 30 minutes (it has a tendency to boil over if covered in the early stages), stirring now and then.

■ Once the mixture has settled down, cover the saucepan and simmer for 2 hours 30 minutes. Stir every half hour or so and add a little more water if the mixture dries out.

■ There should only be enough water left at the end of the cooking to make the mixture into a thickish puree.

■ Keeping the saucepan on the heat, stir in the garlic, ginger and chilies followed by the polenta and continue to cook for 4–5 minutes. Turn off the heat.

■ The mixture now needs to be turned into a coarse puree. As the greens will be very soft, it is possible to puree them by stirring vigorously with a large wooden spoon. If you have a hand blender, it is even easier. Insert the blender into the mixture and switch on briefly. Move the blender around in the pan until all the mixture is pureed. Don't worry if it is a little runny, as the saag will thicken on cooling.

■ Cool the saag, divide into portions and freeze if desired.

Note: If you can't buy spring greens, mustard greens or purple sprouting broccoli, increase the quantities of the other ingredients or try Swiss chard, kale or cabbage.

DHABA-STYLE LAMB CURRY

Dhaba is the Indian word for a Punjabi family restaurant. The Dhaba curry is the basic traditional nonvegetarian curry of north India and is usually made with goat meat. It includes diced meat simmered until meltingly tender along with pieces of bone. Diners can be seen enthusiastically sucking on the bones at these Dhabas. I have provided the traditional recipe which requires some lamb pieces with bone left in, but you can use meat cooked as for lamb curries (page 71) along with some lamb or beef stock if you want to save time.

SERVES 6

Preparation and cooking time:
Step 1:
1¹/₂–1³/₄ hours

Step 1: Preparing the meat
2 tbsp olive oil
1 lb 2 oz (500 g) leg of lamb with bone in, cut into approx. 2-inch (5 cm) pieces
1 lb (450 g) boned leg of lamb, cut slightly larger than 1-inch (2.5 cm) chunks

2 red onions, sliced
2 tsp salt
1 can (14 oz or 400 g) of chopped tomatoes

- Heat half the oil in a large, heavy-based saucepan and add half the meat. Stir-fry until brown. Remove and repeat with the remainder of the meat.

- Return the browned meat to the pan and add the onions. Stir-fry on high heat for about 5 minutes. Turn down the heat, mix in the salt and add the tomatoes. Bring to a boil, cover the pan and simmer on low heat for about 1 hour and 15 minutes or until the meat is tender and the onions have dissolved.

- Use immediately, or cool and refrigerate or freeze for later use.

Preparation and cooking time:
Step 2:
20–25 minutes

Step 2: Preparing the curry
2 tbsp olive oil
4 cloves of garlic
2-inch (5 cm) piece of ginger
    (or 2 portions of prepared garlic-and-ginger mix, page 30, thawed)
2 green chilies, finely chopped
    (or half a portion of prepared green chilies, page 30)

1 tsp chili powder
¹/₂ tsp turmeric
1 tsp cumin powder
1 tsp coriander powder
2 tsp ground ginger
1 tsp paprika
15 fl oz (425 mL) curry sauce (page 32)
2 tsp garam masala

- Heat the oil in a large, heavy-based saucepan and add the garlic, ginger and chilies. Stir-fry for a minute and add the remaining spices (except for the paprika and garam masala), mix well and stir-fry for a minute.

- Add the cooked meat and juices and stir well to coat with spices. Stir-fry on medium to high heat for about 5 minutes. Cover and allow the meat to simmer in the spices for 5–6 minutes on very low heat.

- Add the paprika and the curry sauce and bring to a boil. Simmer, uncovered, for 10 minutes. Stir in the garam masala and serve.

YOGURT CURRY

It may be hard to imagine a curry made from yogurt, but this is in fact quite a substantial (and incredibly tasty) dish popular throughout India. In more recent times it has been making an appearance in Indian restaurants, though generally as a "sauce" with chicken, fish or vegetables. Try it with rice or chapatis; it is quite delicious and simple to make.

If you can, leave the yogurt out of the fridge overnight to sour slightly. You won't need to use any lemon juice if you do that.

SERVES 4–6	
Preparation and cooking time: 1 hour	

13 fl oz (350 mL) plain yogurt
3 tbsp chickpea flour (besan)
2 tsp salt
25 fl oz/1 1/2 US pints (700 mL) cold water
3 tbsp olive oil
1 tsp fenugreek seeds
1 tsp whole black peppercorns
1 tsp whole cumin seeds
6 curry leaves (optional)
1 onion, sliced
4 spring onions, chopped
4 green garlic tops, chopped (optional)

2 cloves of garlic
1-inch (2.5 cm) piece of ginger
    (or a portion of prepared garlic-and-ginger mix, page 30, thawed)
2 green chilies, finely chopped (or half a portion of prepared chilies, page 30)
2 tsp turmeric
1 potato, cut into chunks
4 whole green chilies
1 tsp garam masala
2 tbsp chopped cilantro
juice of half a lemon

TIP

For a variation, add onion, spinach (*palak*) or vegetable pakoras (see tips, page 46) to the finished yogurt curry.

■ In a large bowl, whisk together the yogurt, chickpea flour, salt and water.

■ Heat the oil in a large, heavy-based saucepan, and add the fenugreek seeds, peppercorns, cumin seeds and curry leaves if you are using them. Fry for a few seconds until the seeds start to pop.

■ Add the onion, spring onions and garlic tops if you are using them, and fry on medium heat for 3 minutes. Stir in the garlic, ginger and chilies, and stir-fry for a couple of minutes.

■ Stir in the turmeric and add the potato and whole chilies. Stir around for a minute and pour in the yogurt mixture. Bring to a boil and simmer over low heat for about 30–35 minutes, stirring frequently, until the potato is cooked through.

■ Stir in the garam masala, cilantro and lemon juice if you are using it. Serve with rice or chapati (roti).

ACHARI GHOST

Strong and spicy flavors are the keynotes of this dish. It is traditionally made with mutton simmered long and slow, but this recipe uses precooked lamb, making it a quick and simple dish.

SERVES 4	3 tbsp olive oil	1/2 tsp turmeric
	4 whole red chilies	1 tsp chili powder
Preparation and cooking time: 20–25 minutes	1 tsp cumin seeds	4 tbsp plain yogurt
	1/2 tsp black mustard seeds	15 fl oz (425 mL) curry sauce (page 32)
	1/2 tsp onion seeds	1/2 tsp salt
	1/2 tsp fenugreek seeds	1 lb (450 g) precooked lamb (page 71)
	1/2 tsp fennel seeds	

■ Heat the oil in a large, heavy-based frying pan and stir in the chilies and all the spice seeds. Cook for a few seconds on high heat until the seeds start to pop, and add the turmeric and chili powder.

■ Stir in the yogurt and continue to stir on high heat for a minute or two until the yogurt bubbles and reduces.

■ Add the curry sauce and salt, bring to a boil and stir in the cooked lamb.

■ Turn down the heat and simmer for 10–15 minutes until the sauce is thick and the oil has separated to the surface.

■ Serve simmering hot with rice.

Punjabi Cabbage

Fresh and spicy, this dish is a favorite in northern India. An excellent accompaniment to rich meat curries, yogurt and chapatis, it is simple to make and delicious served hot or cold. Make sure you use good-quality, fresh cabbage.

SERVES 4–6

Preparation and cooking time: 30 minutes

4 tbsp olive oil
1 small onion, sliced
1 tsp cumin seeds
2 cloves of garlic, finely chopped
1-inch (2.5 cm) piece of ginger, finely chopped
  (or a portion of prepared garlic-and-ginger mix,
  page 30, thawed)

2 green chilies, finely chopped (or a portion of
  prepared chilies, page 30)
1 tsp turmeric
1 lb 2 oz (500 g) cabbage, sliced
1 1/2 tsp salt
1 tsp garam masala

■ Heat the oil in a large, heavy-based frying pan or wok and add the onion. Fry for a few minutes while stirring until the onion is transparent.

■ Stir in the cumin seeds and fry for a minute. Add the garlic, ginger and chilies, and stir-fry for a minute or two until aromatic.

■ Stir in the turmeric, followed by the cabbage. Stir-fry the cabbage on medium to high heat for 2 or 3 minutes and add in about 2 tablespoons of water and the salt.

■ Turn down the heat a little and cook the cabbage for another 15 minutes, stirring frequently and adding a little more water if required to prevent it sticking to the bottom of the pan and burning.

■ Stir in the garam masala and serve.

SHIKARI GHOST

Shikari is the Indian word for hunter and this easy-to-cook dish from the Raj era is based on the cooking style of the shikaris when on a hunt. In its simplest form it is large pieces of fresh meat, rubbed with lime juice and hot spices, browned in ghee and simmered in salt and water until tender. The restaurant version includes some onion-based sauce and fresh herbs.

Cook this dish on a day when you have some time to putter around the kitchen because, although it is simple to make, the meat takes a bit of time to cook and it does not freeze well.

SERVES 6–8	Step 1: Preparing the meat	2 tbsp lime juice
Preparation and cooking time: Step 1: 2–2½ hours	1 tsp cumin seeds 1 tsp coriander seeds 1 tsp cardamom 1 tsp cloves 1-inch (2.5 cm) stick of cinnamon 2 lb 4 oz (1 kg) lamb shoulder, cut into large pieces	3 tbsp olive oil 1 tsp ground ginger 2 tsp chili powder 14 fl oz (400 mL) boiling water 2 tsp salt

- Grind the whole spices to a fine powder in an electric grinder or with a pestle and mortar.

- Rinse the meat and drain well. Add the lime juice, 1 tablespoon of the oil and all the spices, and, using your hands, rub well into the meat. Allow to stand for about 10 minutes.

- Heat another tablespoon of oil in a large, heavy-based saucepan and add half the meat. Stir-fry on high heat until well browned. Remove from the pan and repeat with the remaining oil and meat.

- Return all the meat to the pan, add the water and salt and bring to a boil. Simmer, stirring occasionally, for about 2 hours until the meat is tender. Most of the liquid should have evaporated.

- Skim off excess fat, and use immediately or cool and refrigerate for up to 24 hours. For best results, do not freeze as the lovely spice flavors dull with freezing.

Preparation and cooking time: 30 minutes	Step 2: Preparing the curry	33 fl oz/2 US pints (950 mL) curry sauce (page 32)
	1 tbsp olive oil	1 tsp chopped cilantro

- Heat the oil in a large, heavy-based frying pan and stir in the curry sauce. Bring to a boil and add the meat and juices.

- Simmer gently for 15–20 minutes until the sauce is very thick. Stir in the cilantro and serve.

14. PORK AND BEEF DISHES

IN THE HINDU world of 900 million followers the cow is sacred; a divine creature to be esteemed and revered, not butchered and eaten. Even some of the Muslim kings who ruled India in long-ago times prohibited their subjects from eating beef as it was considered offensive to the Hindus. Later, the newly emerging Sikh religion adopted the Hindu belief on the same basis and Sikhs too regard the cow as holy.

Mahatma Gandhi once wrote: "If someone were to ask me what the most important outward manifestation of Hinduism was, I would suggest that it was the idea of cow protection."

From a source of milk to a provider of labor and religious inspiration, cows have played a pivotal role in the Indian way of life for many centuries. Indeed, in India a citizen can be sent to jail for killing or injuring a cow.

There are also religious restrictions on the consumption of pork. Islamic dietary laws forbid the eating of pork, believing it to be "unclean," a harbinger of a multitude of diseases and a degrader of the character, morality and spirituality of the consumer.

There are, nevertheless, states in India that breed, sell and eat both pork and beef. Goa and Kerala on the west coast, supported by a high level of religious tolerance, readily consume pork and beef cooked in traditional vindaloos and bafaths as well as in European-style dishes.

Throughout the West, Sikhs and Hindus consume pork and pork products and Muslims beef. Understandably, Indian restaurants in the West generally have few, if any, pork or beef dishes on the menu. Here are a few traditional and tasty dishes to try at home.

PREPARING BEEF

Tougher cuts of meat require longer cooking but are tastier. I suggest using braising or stewing steak for these recipes but you can use rump if desired.

2 tbsp olive oil
2 lb 4 oz (1 kg) braising beef cut into
   approx. 2-inch (5 cm) pieces
2 onions, sliced
2 tsp salt

Heat half the oil in a large, heavy-based saucepan and add half the meat. Stir-fry until brown. Remove and repeat with the remainder of the meat.

Return the browned meat to the pan and add the onions. Stir-fry on high heat for about five minutes. Turn down the heat and stir in the salt.

Cover the pan with a tight-fitting lid and simmer on low heat for about 1½ hours or until the meat is tender and the onions have dissolved.

Use immediately, or cool and refrigerate or freeze for later use.

Beef dishes

Massaman Curry
Slow-cooked chunks of beef in a rich, creamy sauce, mildly spiced.

Beef Vindaloo
The fabulously fiery flavors of the old Portuguese settlement of Goa. Hot and tangy, this dish is a delicious balance of pungent and aromatic spices.

Bombay Beef
Street food of Bombay (now Mumbai), this combination of diced beef and potatoes is cooked in a sauce enriched with coconut milk and flavored with spices.

Beef Badami
Mild beef curry with tender chunks of meat combined with aromatic spices and almonds, finished with a touch of cream.

MASSAMAN CURRY

This is a dish more common in Thai restaurants, but I've included it because it originated with the Muslim community in India and because it is absolutely delicious. Unlike neighboring countries, Thailand managed to remain free from colonization by European powers and, as a result, its food has limited outside influences. The Thais have, however, borrowed cooking styles from other countries such as China, India and Malaysia, and Massaman Curry is a stunning example of this.

Massaman curry paste is readily available from supermarkets and Asian grocers and is relatively good. If you would like to go a step further, I have included the recipe so you can make your own.

SERVES 4	2 tbsp olive oil	18 fl oz/1 US pint (500 mL) coconut cream
	2 tsp grated ginger	18 fl oz/1 US pint (500 mL) coconut milk
Preparation and cooking time: 30 minutes	1/2 tsp ground cumin	1 tbsp palm sugar or soft brown sugar
	4 tbsp Massaman paste	3 tbsp fish sauce
	6 green cardamom pods, crushed	2 tsp tamarind paste dissolved in 2 tbsp warm water
	1-inch (2.5 cm) stick of cinnamon	1 lb (450 g) precooked beef (page 111)
	3 oz (100 g) peanuts	

MAKE YOUR OWN MASSAMAN PASTE

12 dried chilies, deseeded and soaked
1 whole garlic bulb, cloves peeled
2 oz (60 g) sliced shallots
1 tbsp ground coriander
1 tsp ground cumin
1 tsp ground pepper
1 tsp lemongrass, chopped
1-inch (2.5 cm) piece of galangal, peeled, chopped
1 tsp kaffir lime zest
1 tbsp scraped, chopped cilantro roots
3 tsp salt
1 tsp shrimp paste (belacan)
2 tbsp olive oil

Grind or process all the ingredients until you have a fairly smooth paste. Place in a clean jar, pour a little oil over the top and keep in the fridge for up to a week.

■ Heat the oil in a wok or heavy-based saucepan and add the ginger and cumin. Stir-fry for a few seconds and add the Massaman paste, cardamoms, cinnamon and peanuts. Stir-fry for 2 minutes.

■ Stir in half the coconut cream and bring to a simmer. Cook on medium heat, stirring often, until the cream is completely absorbed into the paste and the oil starts to separate from the mixture. Repeat with the remaining coconut cream.

■ Stir in the coconut milk and bring to a simmer. Simmer, stirring often, for about 10 minutes until the sauce has reduced.

■ Stir in the sugar, fish sauce, tamarind and meat. Bring back to simmer and cook on low heat for another 10 minutes. Do not boil vigorously as the coconut sauce may separate.

■ Serve with rice and chapatis.

Beef Vindaloo

Vindaloo is the Portuguese name for vinegar and garlic. Perhaps it should be vinegar and chili because vindaloo is notorious for being hot, hot, hot, and for some, the hotter the better. However, for a good vindaloo, the heat should be balanced with other spicy flavors.

Traditionally, a combination of clear and dark vinegars is often used to make vindaloo. The clear vinegar is made from coconut and the dark from molasses. Balsamic vinegar works well.

SERVES 4	4 cloves of garlic, finely chopped	2 tbsp dark balsamic vinegar
Preparation and cooking time: 20 minutes	1-inch (2.5 cm) piece of ginger, grated or julienned 2 green chilies, finely sliced (or half a portion of prepared chili, page 30) 1¹/2 tsp garam masala ¹/2 tsp turmeric 1 tsp chili powder or to taste	3 tbsp olive oil 15 fl oz (425 mL) curry sauce (page 32) ¹/2 tsp salt 1 lb (450 g) precooked beef (page 111) ¹/2 tsp dried ground fenugreek leaves (optional)

■ In a small bowl, mix together the garlic, ginger, chilies, 1 teaspoon of the garam masala, turmeric, chili powder and vinegar.

■ Heat the oil in a deep, heavy-based frying pan and add the spice mix. Stir-fry for about a minute or until aromatic.

■ Add the curry sauce and salt and bring to a boil. Cook on high for about 5 minutes until thickened.

■ Add the meat and bring back to a simmer. Stir in the remainder of the garam masala and fenugreek leaves, if you are using them. Simmer for 5 minutes or until the oil separates from the sauce.

■ Serve.

BOMBAY BEEF

From the streets of Bombay (officially Mumbai, since 1995) comes this delicious combination of tender beef and potato in a beautifully spiced sauce made silky smooth by the addition of a little coconut milk. If you don't have coconut milk in the pantry, evaporated light milk or a little cream will work well.

SERVES 4

Preparation and cooking time: 20 minutes

1 large or 2 small potatoes, peeled and cut into chunks
3 tbsp olive oil
2 tsp tomato paste
$^1/_2$ tsp turmeric
15 fl oz (425 mL) curry sauce (page 32)

1 lb (450 g) precooked beef (page 111)
$^1/_2$ tsp salt
1 tsp chili powder
4 tbsp coconut milk
1 tsp garam masala
1 tsp tamarind dissolved in 1 tbsp warm water

■ Cook the potato in boiling salted water for about 10 minutes until just tender. Drain.

■ Meanwhile, heat the oil in a deep, heavy-based frying pan and stir in the tomato paste and turmeric. Stir around in the hot oil for 10 seconds and add the curry sauce.

■ Bring to a boil and cook on high for about 5 minutes until the sauce is thick and starting to release the oil.

■ Stir in the beef, salt, chili powder, cooked potato and coconut milk. Bring back to a boil and simmer gently for about 10 minutes, stirring often.

■ Add the garam masala and tamarind, simmer for a minute, and serve.

BEEF BADAMI

A mildly spiced but flavorsome dish, Beef Badami is inspired by rich Mughal influences. The ground almonds and cream make for a deliciously creamy sauce while the lightly toasted flaked almonds add a contrasting crunch. A tasty and impressive dish fit for a king.

SERVES 4

Preparation and cooking time: 20–25 minutes

2 tbsp olive oil
4 cardamom pods
1-inch (2.5 cm) stick of cinnamon
3 cloves
1/2 tsp ground cumin
1 tsp ground coriander
15 fl oz (425 mL) curry sauce (page 32)

1/2 tsp salt
1/2 tsp chili powder
1 lb (450 g) precooked beef (page 111)
1 oz (30 g) almonds, ground to a fine powder
5 fl oz (150 mL) light cream
1 tbsp sliced or slivered almonds, toasted

■ Heat the oil in a deep, heavy-based frying pan and add the cardamom, cinnamon and cloves. Stir-fry on medium heat for a minute, add the cumin and coriander, and fry for a few seconds more.

■ Add the curry sauce, salt and chili powder, and bring to a boil. Cook on high heat, stirring, for about 5 minutes until the sauce thickens.

■ Stir in the beef and ground almonds. Bring back to a boil and simmer for 5 or 6 minutes, stirring often. Add the cream and simmer for another 3 minutes.

■ Serve sprinkled with the sliced or slivered toasted almonds.

Pork dishes

Pork Tikka
Marinated chunks of pork fillet, encrusted with toasty spices on the outside and tender and juicy on the inside.

Mangalorean-style Pork Bafath
Boneless pork in an aromatic mix of roasted spices, south Indian style.

Pork and Sprouts
A tasty combination of tender pork fillet and fresh brussels sprouts simmered in a spicy sauce until they melt in the mouth.

Chili Pork
Juicy strips of pork with green and red chilies in a tangy, flavorsome sauce.

PORK TIKKA

Another Punjabi delicacy regularly enjoyed at Punjabi roadside restaurants (or Dhabas), this dish has little in common with the chicken dish of the same name. It is robustly spiced, though not too hot, very easy to cook and extremely good. Pork Tikka can be served as a main course with a yogurt dish to temper the spices, or as an appetizer with a crisp salad.

SERVES 3–4 as a main course and 6–8 as an appetizer

Preparation and cooking time: 22 minutes (plus marinating time)

Marinade
1 onion
4 cloves of garlic
2-inch (5 cm) piece of ginger
2 green chilies
1 tsp ground cumin
1 tsp ground coriander
5 fl oz (150 mL) plain yogurt
1 tbsp olive oil

1 lb (450 g) pork fillet
4 tbsp olive oil
1/2 tsp turmeric
15 fl oz (425 mL) curry sauce (page 32)
1 tsp paprika
1 tsp salt
3 tsp garam masala
1 tbsp chopped cilantro

■ Process or finely chop the onion, garlic, ginger and chilies and combine with the remaining marinade ingredients.

■ Trim the pork fillet and slice into 1-inch (2.5 cm) chunks. Place in a bowl with the marinade, cover and refrigerate for about 2 hours or overnight. Remove from the fridge about 30 minutes before using.

- Heat half the oil in a deep, heavy-based frying pan, add the turmeric, stir once and add the curry sauce. Bring to a boil and cook for about 5 minutes until thick.

- Turn down the heat, stir in the paprika and salt, and simmer gently while cooking the pork.

- Heat the remaining oil in a karahi or large frying pan, and add the meat and marinade. Stir-fry on high for 3–4 minutes until the liquid has evaporated and the meat is starting to brown.

- Add the meat mixture to the sauce, scraping out all the crusty pieces that will have stuck to the pan. Stir-fry again on high for 3–4 minutes.

- Turn down the heat and simmer, stirring often, for about 15 minutes or until all the liquid has evaporated and the mixture is rich and dark.

- Stir in the garam masala and stir-fry on low heat for a minute or two. Serve sprinkled with the cilantro.

MANGALOREAN-STYLE PORK BAFATH

Mangalore is an Indian coastal state south of Goa. Its cuisine is a product of many influences, including those of Goa, Portugal and the Middle East. This dish is based on the Mangalorean style of cooking with the abundant use of roasted spices for aroma and flavor, and the use of tamarind and vinegar for balance and a tasty tang. It doesn't have the heat of the Goan vindaloos, so the flavor of the spices really shines through.

SERVES 3–4	Spice mix for roasting	Remaining ingredients
	1 tsp coriander seeds	1 lb (450 g) pork fillet
Preparation and cooking time: 35–40 minutes	1/2 tsp cumin seeds	4 tbsp olive oil
	4 dried red chilies	1 tsp tamarind paste dissolved in 1 tbsp warm water
	6 black peppercorns	1 onion, thinly sliced
	1-inch (2.5 cm) stick of cinnamon	1 clove garlic, thinly sliced
	2 cloves	15 fl oz (425 mL) curry sauce (page 32)
	1/2 tsp turmeric	1 tsp salt
	2 black cardamom pods (optional)	1 tsp paprika
		2 tsp dark balsamic vinegar
		1 green chili, finely sliced

■ Roast the spices in a small pan over medium heat for about a minute or until aromatic. Remove from the pan and cool. Grind to a fine powder in a pestle and mortar or electric grinder.

■ Trim the pork fillet and slice into large chunks about 1¼-inch (3 cm) in size. Combine the pork with 1 tablespoon of the oil, the spice mix, tamarind, onion and garlic.

■ Heat the rest of the oil in a deep, heavy-based frying pan and add the curry sauce, salt and paprika. Bring to a boil and cook on high heat for about 5 minutes until thick and starting to release the oil. Lower the heat and simmer gently while cooking the meat.

■ Heat a karahi or frying pan and stir-fry the meat mixture for about 3 minutes until browned. Add the meat to the thickened sauce, scraping the karahi to remove all the crusty pieces, and stir in the vinegar and roast spices.

■ Cover and simmer gently for 10 minutes, stirring once or twice. Remove the lid and simmer for another 10 minutes until the meat is cooked through. Add a little water if the mixture becomes too dry or sticks to the bottom of the pan during this time.

■ Stir in the green chili and serve.

PORK AND BRUSSELS SPROUTS

A Punjabi innovation, this dish combines the richness of pork with the freshness of brussels sprouts, and it is a combination that is incredibly good. Traditionally, the dish would be made with pork shoulder or rib, with lots of bone and fat to "roast" the spices and add plenty of flavor. This recipe uses pork fillet, making it a healthier option, and is quick and easy to prepare. It is only worth making this dish around winter when fresh, sweet brussels sprouts are in season. At other times of the year, try a variation with shredded cabbage or spinach.

SERVES 4

Preparation and cooking time: 30 minutes

14 oz (400 g) pork fillet
4 tbsp olive oil
1 tsp turmeric
2 green chilies, finely sliced (or half a portion of prepared chili, page 30)
2 cloves of garlic, finely sliced
1-inch (2.5 cm) piece of ginger, finely sliced (or a portion of prepared garlic-and-ginger mix, page 30, thawed)

9 oz (250 g) brussels sprouts
2 ripe tomatoes, chopped
1 tsp salt
15 fl oz (425 mL) curry sauce (page 32)
1 tsp garam masala

■ Trim the pork fillet and slice into 1-inch (2.5 cm) pieces. Place in a bowl with 1 tablespoon of the oil, half the turmeric, the chilies, garlic and ginger. Mix well and set aside.

■ Slice off the exposed end of the stalks and remove outer leaves from the brussels sprouts. Rinse under cold water and cut into quarters. Place in a microwave-proof container with 2 tablespoons of water, and microwave on high for 3 minutes.

■ Heat the remaining oil in a deep, heavy-based frying pan and add the tomatoes, salt and remaining turmeric. Cook, stirring for 2 or 3 minutes until the tomato is pulpy.

■ Stir in the pork and stir-fry on medium to high heat for 3 minutes. Add the curry sauce and brussels sprouts to the pan, and bring to a boil, stirring often. Cover the pan and simmer for 10–12 minutes.

■ Remove the lid and simmer for another 5 minutes, stirring often, until the liquid has evaporated.

■ Stir in the garam masala, heat for a minute and serve.

CHILI PORK

A colorful and tasty dish, Chili Pork is inspired by Chinese influences and will appeal to those who relish the flavor and aroma of fresh chilies. By using the larger (often called Thai) chilies, the color and flavor are achieved without the extra heat. Use a combination of hot and mild chilies if you prefer a hotter dish.

SERVES 4

Preparation and cooking time: 30 minutes

1 lb 2 oz (500 g) pork fillet, sliced into strips
2 cloves of garlic, finely sliced
1-inch (2.5 cm) piece of ginger, finely sliced
  (or a portion of prepared garlic-and-ginger mix, page 30, thawed)
$1/2$ tsp turmeric
4 tbsp olive oil
15 fl oz (425 mL) curry sauce (page 32)
$1/2$ tsp chili powder or to taste

1 tsp salt
4 large, mild green chilies, deseeded and sliced into thin strips
4 large, mild red chilies, deseeded and sliced into thin strips
$1/2$ red pepper, thinly sliced
1 ripe tomato, sliced into 8 wedges
$1^1/2$ tsp garam masala
2 tbsp chopped cilantro

■ Combine the pork, garlic, ginger, turmeric and 1 tablespoon of the oil in a bowl.

■ Heat 1 tablespoon of the oil in a deep, heavy-based frying pan and add the pork. Stir-fry the meat for 3 minutes on high. Add the curry sauce, chili powder and salt, and simmer for 10 minutes.

■ Meanwhile, heat the remaining oil in a separate pan and add the sliced chilies and red pepper. Stir-fry on medium heat for 3 minutes until starting to color.

■ Stir the fried chilies and red pepper into the pork mixture and simmer for another 5 minutes before adding the tomato and garam masala.

■ Simmer gently for 5 minutes. The sauce should be very thick and the oil should be separating from the sauce.

■ Serve sprinkled with the cilantro.

15. SEAFOOD DISHES

Fish and seafood dishes are prominent in the coastal states of India, where the Arabian Sea, Bay of Bengal and Indian Ocean yield their rich bounties of fish and shellfish. The entire west coast of India is renowned for its seafood dishes. For people living along the Indian coastline, fried, steamed, curried and even pickled seafood is a firm favorite. Families rise early to reach the fish markets in anticipation of the catch of the day.

Seafood dishes

Shrimp Baadsha with Poori
Jumbo shrimp sautéed with spring onions, sweet peppers and spices, served with a hot, creamy sauce with fried Indian bread (*poori*).

Fish Masala
Juicy fish fillets, marinated and pan-fried, served with a tangy, hot sauce flavored with a touch of yogurt, tomatoes and fresh herbs.

Fish Ambotik
Marinated fillets of fish cooked in a sweet-and-sour sauce flavored with cloves, tamarind and whole red chilies.

Shrimp Malabar
Fresh shrimp cooked with sautéed onions, sweet peppers, tomatoes and coconut, finished with a touch of cream.

Palak Fish
Chunks of fresh fish, spinach leaves and fresh fenugreek, sautéed with onions, tomatoes, cumin seeds and green chili.

Salmon Kalia
A Bengali speciality — whole fillets of fried fish served in a spicy sauce with a touch of yogurt.

Goan Fish Curry
Marinated fish chunks flavored with mustard seeds, curry leaves and whole red chilies, served in a thick coconut sauce.

Shrimp Baadsha with Poori

This is a special-occasion dish that is beautiful to look at and sensational to eat. A delectable dish that was once served in the royal palaces to the reigning kings and princes (*baadshas*), it reflects the flamboyance and decadence of a bygone era. It has a lovely combination of flavors in a deliciously creamy sauce.

SERVES 4	24 jumbo shrimp	15 fl oz (425 mL) curry sauce (page 32)
Preparation and cooking time: 20 minutes	2 spring onions, chopped	1 tsp salt
	2 green garlic tops, chopped (optional)	4 tbsp yogurt
	1/2 red pepper, sliced into strips	4 tbsp thick cream
	1 tsp turmeric	2 tbsp ground almonds
	2 green chilies, finely chopped	1/2 tsp chili powder
	1/2 tsp fennel seeds	1/2 tsp garam masala
	1 tsp ground coriander	1 ripe tomato, sliced into 8 wedges
	3 tbsp olive oil	2 tbsp chopped cilantro
	1-inch (2.5 cm) stick of cinnamon	

■ Shell and devein the shrimp. Rinse, drain and pat dry with paper towels. Combine with the spring onions, garlic tops (if you are using them), red pepper, half the turmeric, chilies, fennel seeds, coriander and 1 tablespoon of the oil. Set aside.

■ Heat the remaining oil in a deep, heavy-based frying pan and add the cinnamon stick and stir for a few seconds. Add the shrimp mixture and stir-fry for about a minute.

■ Stir in the curry sauce and salt, and bring to a boil. Cook on medium heat for about 3 minutes until the sauce thickens slightly. Turn down to a simmer.

■ Stir in the yogurt, cream, almonds and chili powder. Simmer gently for 5 minutes. Stir through the garam masala, tomatoes and half the cilantro. Simmer for a minute.

■ Serve sprinkled with the remaining cilantro accompanied by Poori (page 160).

FISH MASALA

This dish is really quick and easy to prepare and has a lovely creamy and colorful sauce. The key to a really good Fish Masala is to buy the freshest fish you can.

SERVES 4	1 lb 2 oz (500 g) fish fillets (any firm-fleshed	2 tsp tomato paste
	white fish)	15 fl oz (425 mL) curry sauce (page 32)
Preparation and	1 tsp salt	1 green chili, finely sliced
cooking time:	1 tsp turmeric	2 tbsp plain yogurt
20 minutes	1/2 tsp chili powder	4 cherry tomatoes, halved
	3 tbsp olive oil	1/2 tsp garam masala
	2 spring onions, sliced	1 tbsp thick cream
	2 green garlic tops, sliced (optional)	2 tbsp chopped cilantro

- Rinse the fish fillets and pat dry with paper towels. Slice into large chunks.

- Combine half the salt, half the turmeric, the chili powder and 1 tablespoon of the oil with the fish pieces, and set aside.

- Heat the remaining oil in a deep, heavy-based frying pan and add the spring onions and garlic tops (if you are using them). Stir-fry for 3 minutes. Stir in the tomato paste and cook for a minute more.

- Add the curry sauce with the remaining salt and turmeric, and bring to a boil. Cook the sauce on high for about 5 minutes until thickened.

- Stir the chili and yogurt into the sauce and cook, stirring until completely incorporated. Lower the heat and simmer gently while cooking the fish.

- Heat a separate frying pan or karahi and stir-fry the fish on high heat for a minute or two until lightly browned. Add the fish to the sauce and simmer for 5 minutes.

- Stir in the tomatoes, garam masala, cream and half the cilantro. Simmer for a minute and serve sprinkled with the remaining cilantro.

FISH AMBOTIK

This is another south Indian delicacy thought to have originated in Goa that has been modified over time by the Mangaloreans and other southern states. The delicious sauce has the robust flavors of garlic and mustard seeds, and the sour tamarind is balanced by the addition of sugar and a generous amount of chili.

SERVES 4

Preparation and cooking time: 20–25 minutes

1 lb 2 oz (500 g) firm white fish fillets
2 tsp tamarind paste dissolved in 3 fl oz (100 mL) warm water
2 tsp soft brown sugar
1 tsp chili powder
3 tbsp olive oil
$1/2$ tsp black mustard seeds

4 cloves garlic, finely chopped
1 tsp ground cumin
$1/2$ tsp salt
$1/2$ tsp turmeric
1 ripe tomato, chopped
15 fl oz (425 mL) curry sauce (page 32)
4 whole red chilies

■ Rinse the fish, pat dry with paper towels and cut into chunks. Combine the fish, tamarind, sugar and chili powder in a bowl, and set aside.

■ Heat the oil in a deep, heavy-based frying pan and add the mustard seeds. Stir for a few seconds, then add the garlic. Stir-fry for a minute or two and add the cumin, salt and turmeric.

■ Stir in the tomato, cook for a minute and stir in the curry sauce. Bring to a boil and simmer for 5 minutes until thickened slightly.

■ Add the fish and marinade, bring back to a boil and simmer the fish in the sauce for about 5 minutes, stirring carefully, until the fish is cooked through. The sauce should be quite thin.

■ Serve topped with the whole red chilies.

SHRIMP MALABAR

Although Malabar is a region in the southern state of India where food is generally more fiery and pungent, Malabar cuisine is noted for its mild flavors and gentle cooking styles such as steaming or baking. The subtle spicing in this dish is ideally suited to the delicate flavor of fresh shrimp. If you are using frozen shrimp, thaw in the fridge overnight and pat dry before using.

SERVES 4

Preparation and cooking time: 20–25 minutes

Spice mix
1 tbsp coriander seeds
1 tbsp poppy seeds
1 tbsp grated coconut (or shredded coconut)
1-inch (2.5 cm) stick of cinnamon
2 cloves
4 green cardamom pods

1 lb 2 oz (500 g) shelled fresh or frozen shrimp
3 tbsp olive oil
2 tbsp sliced onion
1/2 red pepper, sliced
1/2 tsp turmeric
15 fl oz (425 mL) curry sauce (page 32)
1 tsp salt
6 cherry tomatoes, halved
1 green chili, finely sliced
1 tbsp thick cream
1 tbsp chopped cilantro

■ Grind the spices and coconut to a fine powder in a pestle and mortar or electric grinder. Combine with the shrimp and 1 tablespoon of oil. Set aside.

■ Heat the remaining oil in a deep, heavy-based frying pan and add the onion and red pepper. Stir-fry for 3 minutes until soft and add the turmeric, curry sauce and salt.

■ Bring to a boil and cook on high for 5 minutes until thickened. Turn down the heat and let the sauce simmer very gently.

■ Meanwhile, heat a separate pan or karahi and stir-fry the shrimp on medium heat for about 2 minutes. Add to the sauce and simmer for 2 minutes. Stir in the tomatoes and simmer for another 3 or 4 minutes.

■ Finally, stir in the green chili and cream. Cook gently for another 2 minutes and serve, sprinkled with the cilantro.

PALAK FISH

This is a tasty dish originating in the north of India where fresh fenugreek is used in abundance. The distinct "curryish" flavor of the fenugreek beautifully enhances the relatively mild flavor of the fish and spinach in this dish.

SERVES 4	1 lb 2 oz (500 g) firm-fleshed white fish	4 oz (125 g) spinach leaves, shredded
Preparation and cooking time: 20–25 minutes	3 tbsp olive oil 1 tsp cumin seeds 1 onion, sliced 2 cloves of garlic, finely sliced 2 ripe tomatoes, sliced	4 oz (125 g) fresh fenugreek leaves, shredded 7 fl oz (200 mL) curry sauce (page 32) 1 tsp salt 2 green chilies, finely sliced

- Rinse the fish fillets, pat dry with paper towels and cut into large chunks.

- Heat the oil in a deep, heavy-based frying pan and add the cumin seeds. Stir-fry for a few seconds and add the onion and garlic. Fry on high heat for 2–3 minutes until soft.

- Add half the tomatoes and stir around in the hot oil for about a minute before adding the spinach and fenugreek.

- Stir-fry on high heat for about 3 minutes. Turn down the heat and cook for another 5 minutes, stirring now and then, until the mixture is quite dry.

- Add the curry sauce and salt and bring to a boil. Simmer for 5 minutes.

- Stir in the fish and chilies and simmer, uncovered, for another 10–12 minutes, stirring carefully, until the fish is cooked through and the liquid has almost evaporated.

- Stir through the remaining tomatoes and serve.

SALMON KALIA

This is a wonderful Bengali delicacy traditionally made with a carplike fish called *katla*. The delicious aromatically spiced sauce is flavored with a special spice blend called *panch phoran* (five spices), which complements the oily fish beautifully. Salmon is an excellent substitute for the traditional katla but other varieties of fish can also be used.

SERVES 4

Preparation and cooking time: 20–25 minutes

Spice blend
1/2 tsp fenugreek seeds
1 tsp black mustard seeds
1 tsp onion seeds
1 tsp fennel seeds
2 tsp cumin seeds

Remaining ingredients
1 tsp turmeric
1 1/2 tsp salt
4 salmon cutlets or fillets about 7 oz (200 g) each

2 tbsp olive oil
1 clove of garlic, finely sliced
2 tsp tomato paste
20 fl oz (600 mL) curry sauce (page 32)
1 tsp paprika
3 tbsp plain yogurt
1 ripe tomato, sliced into 8 wedges (or 4 cherry tomatoes, halved)
2 hot red chilies, deseeded and sliced
1/2 tsp garam masala
2 tbsp chopped cilantro

■ Combine all the spices for the spice blend and set aside. Mix half the turmeric with half the salt and rub over the fish. Set aside.

■ Heat the oil in a deep, heavy-based frying pan and add the spice blend. Stir around in the hot oil for about 20 seconds until the seeds start to pop, then add the garlic. Fry for another few seconds and stir in the tomato paste and remaining turmeric.

■ Stir-fry for a minute and add the curry sauce, paprika and the remaining salt. Bring to a boil and cook on high for 2 minutes until slightly thickened. Turn down the heat and stir in the yogurt. Simmer while preparing the fish.

■ Heat a separate pan capable of holding all the fish in a single layer. Cook on high heat for a minute each side or until lightly browned.

■ Transfer the fish to the sauce and turn the pieces in the sauce until each piece is completely coated.

■ Bring to a boil and turn down the heat. Cover and simmer for 10–15 minutes, turning once. Stir in the tomato halfway through.

■ Transfer to a serving platter or plates, sprinkle with the red chilies, garam masala and cilantro. Serve.

Note: This dish needs the extra sauce to counterbalance the richness of the fish.

GOAN FISH CURRY

A traditional fish curry from Goa that like most Goan food, is colorful, hot and delicious. This is a quick and easy recipe that doesn't require any curry sauce — the spice mix and coconut milk combine to make a delicious thick sauce. Reduce the number of chilies if you don't want it too hot.

Use any fish of your choice. Tuna and salmon work well with this dish, as does any firm-fleshed white fish.

SERVES 4

Preparation and cooking time: 20–25 minutes

Bengali Panch Phoran (Bengali five-spice mix)
8 dried red chilies
2 tsp cumin seeds
3 tsp coriander seeds
1 tsp black mustard seeds
1 tsp fenugreek seeds

Remaining ingredients
1 lb 2 oz (500 g) fish, cut into large chunks
2 tsp tamarind dissolved in 2 tbsp warm water
1 tsp salt
1 tsp turmeric
2 tbsp olive oil

1 onion, sliced
4 curry leaves
2 cloves garlic, ground to a paste
1-inch (2.5 cm) piece of ginger
    (or a portion of prepared garlic-and-ginger
    mix, page 30, thawed)
1 ripe tomato, chopped
1/2 tsp paprika
10 fl oz (300 mL) coconut milk
3 fl oz (100 mL) coconut cream
4 red chilies, slit and deseeded
1/2 tsp garam masala

■ Combine the spices for the spice mix and grind to a fine powder in a pestle and mortar or electric grinder. Set aside.

■ Combine the fish with the tamarind, half the salt and half the turmeric, and set aside.

■ Heat the oil in a deep, heavy-based frying pan and add the sliced onion. Stir-fry for 4–5 minutes until lightly browned and stir in the curry leaves, spice mix, remaining salt and turmeric. Fry for a few seconds.

■ Add the garlic and ginger. Stir-fry for a minute until aromatic and add the tomato. Cook the tomato for a couple of minutes until pulpy and stir in the paprika, coconut milk and cream.

■ Bring to a boil and simmer for about 5 minutes until thickened slightly. Stir in the red chilies, fish and marinade, bring back to a simmer and cook for 10 minutes, stirring once or twice until the fish is cooked through.

■ Serve sprinkled with garam masala.

16. VEGETABLE AND DHAL DISHES

I T IS VIRTUALLY impossible for a Westerner to imagine sitting down to a good meal without a generous portion of meat, chicken or fish. Yet 70 percent of the population of the Indian subcontinent is vegetarian and does just that.

Historically, Indian cuisine has been shaped by many influences, the most significant of which is probably vegetarianism, largely brought about by strong religious beliefs beginning with Buddhism and Jainism, which came to India around 600 BCE. Although these are no longer major religions in India they had the effect of pervading Indian culture and converting its people to a way of life where consuming flesh is strictly against their faith (*dharam*).

There is some scientific evidence to suggest that non-meat-eating populations have a lower life expectancy, although there is little to support this in areas where food is fresh and plentiful and poverty and famine do not play a role. Indian vegetarian food is so varied and diverse that it is easy to get sufficient nutrients, protein and fiber without high levels of fat, a balance often lacking in modern Western diets. Fresh, homemade yogurt or curd is eaten at every meal, providing good quality protein and plenty of vitamins and minerals. Pulses, lentils or chickpeas feature daily and, eaten with bread or rice, provide complete proteins and lots of fiber. The addition of fresh or sun-dried herbs and spices gives further nutritional value to the dishes. Even snacks and desserts, often made with besan (chickpea flour) and milk, are nutritious. Indian vegetarian food is also delicious due to the myriad of spices, pickles, chutneys and relishes that are consumed at each meal. With this wonderful cuisine it is possible to eat vegetarian dishes every day and not miss eating meat. Indeed, India is quite a paradise for vegetarians.

Even if you are not vegetarian, the following dishes are good accompaniments that add variety and interest to the meat dishes in the preceding chapters.

Vegetable and dhal dishes

Cauliflower Keema
Minced cauliflower cooked with fennel seeds, garlic, ginger and peas. A deliciously "meaty" dish.

Aloo Soy "Bari"
Potato and meaty soy chunks in a deliciously spicy gravy flavored with fresh herbs.

Bengan Ka Bharta
Roasted, skinless eggplant, finely chopped into a coarse puree and sautéed with onions, tomatoes, spices and herbs.

Palak Paneer Kasoori
Indian cheese cubes, panfried until crisp and tossed with spinach, sun-dried fenugreek leaves, onions, ginger and cumin.

Shabnam Curry
Mushrooms, potatoes, peas and cashew nuts cooked in an authentic combination of garlic, ginger and onion flavored with fresh cilantro.

Hatho Brinjal
A spicy combination of eggplant, potatoes and peas, cooked with fresh tomatoes and shredded coconut.

Tarka Dhal
A quick-cook version of this popular dhal, lightly spiced and generously flavored with fresh herbs.

CAULIFLOWER KEEMA

This is a quick and simple recipe, good as a main dish, or as a side dish with a dhal or meat curry. As with most recipes, fresh cauliflower that is in season will produce the best results. If you can get it, try it with organic cauliflower — it is even better.

SERVES 4–6

Preparation and cooking time: 30 minutes

1 small cauliflower
3 tbsp olive oil
1/2 tsp fennel seeds
1 ripe tomato, chopped
1 tsp salt
1/2 tsp turmeric

1 green chili, finely sliced
13 fl oz (350 mL) curry sauce (page 32)
5 oz (150 g) frozen peas
1/2 tsp garam masala
1 tbsp chopped cilantro

■ Break the cauliflower into florets. Rinse and drain well. Place into a food processor and process on slow speed until coarsely minced. Alternatively, grate or chop finely.

■ Heat the oil in a heavy-based pan and add the fennel seeds, tomato, salt and turmeric. Cook on medium heat for about 2 minutes and stir in the green chili.

■ Cook for about a minute before adding the cauliflower. Stir for 3–4 minutes on medium heat and add the curry sauce.

■ Bring to a boil and simmer for 15 minutes, stirring occasionally, until the liquid has almost evaporated and the cauliflower is tender.

■ Stir in the peas and garam masala, and cook for another 5 minutes, stirring often.

■ Serve sprinkled with the cilantro.

ALOO SOY "BARI"

This has become a popular dish among Indian vegetarian populations in recent years. Textured vegetable protein (TVP; also known as soy chunks or nuggets) is highly nutritious and is an excellent substitute for meat. Because it readily absorbs the flavors of the sauce, it becomes very tasty too. It is quite unlike the traditional *bari* which can be described as a spicy, sun-dried "cake" of fermented ground mung dahl, but it is a convenient and delicious alternative. TVP is available from Indian grocers, health food stores and some supermarkets.

SERVES 4

Preparation and cooking time: 30 minutes

11 oz (300 g) TVP
2 medium potatoes
3 tbsp olive oil
2 spring onions, chopped
1 tbsp chopped fenugreek leaves (optional)
2 green chilies, finely chopped
1/2 tsp cumin seeds

1/2 tsp turmeric
15 fl oz (425 mL) curry sauce (page 32)
1 tsp salt
14 fl oz (400 mL) hot water
1 tsp garam masala
2 tbsp chopped cilantro

■ Soak the TVP in enough hot water to cover. Set aside.

■ Peel the potatoes and slice each one into 6 or 8 evenly sized chunks. Boil in salted water for about 10 minutes until just tender but not breaking apart. Drain.

■ Meanwhile, heat the oil in a deep, heavy-based frying pan and fry the spring onion (and fenugreek leaves if you are using them) for about 2 minutes.

■ Add the chilies, cumin seeds and turmeric, fry for 30 seconds and stir in the curry sauce and salt. Bring to a boil and cook on medium to high heat for about 5 minutes, stirring frequently until the sauce is thick.

■ Add the drained TVP and about 14 fl oz (400 mL) of hot water. Bring to a boil and simmer partly covered for 10 minutes.

■ Add the potatoes and garam masala, and simmer for another 5 minutes. Stir in the chopped cilantro and serve.

BENGAN KA BHARTA

Native to India, the eggplant (*bengan* or *brinjal*) is used widely in Indian cuisine. Its incredible versatility allows it to be used in a huge variety of different ways from pickles to curries. Bengan Ka Bharta is another delicious example of the versatility of this king of vegetables. Traditionally, the eggplants would be roasted in the dying embers of the cooking fire, but microwaving is a quick option.

For this dish, choose large eggplants with a smooth, shiny skin and bright green stalks.

SERVES 4–6	2 large eggplants (they should weigh about 1 lb 12 oz or 800 g in total)	2 green chilies, finely chopped (or a portion of prepared chili, page 30)
Preparation and cooking time: 40 minutes	4 tbsp olive oil	2 ripe tomatoes, chopped
	1 onion, finely chopped	$1^{1}/_{2}$ tsp salt
	1 tsp cumin seeds	$^{1}/_{2}$ tsp turmeric
	2 cloves of garlic, finely chopped	1 tsp garam masala
	1-inch (2.5 cm) piece of ginger, finely chopped (or a portion of prepared garlic-and-ginger mix, page 30, thawed)	2 tbsp chopped cilantro

■ Make 3 or 4 large slits along the length of the eggplants and microwave on high for 3 minutes. Turn the eggplants over and microwave again for 2 or 3 minutes or until the vegetables are quite soft. Remember they will continue cooking once the microwave is off. Alternatively, roast in a hot oven at 425°F (220°C) for about 35 minutes. Allow to stand until cool enough to handle.

■ Meanwhile, heat the oil in a deep, heavy-based frying pan and fry the onion and cumin for 3 or 4 minutes until the onion softens.

■ Add the garlic, ginger and chilies, and stir-fry for a minute. Add the tomatoes, salt and turmeric, and cook over low heat for about 10 minutes until the tomatoes are pulpy and the oil starts to separate from the mixture.

■ Meanwhile, peel the eggplants and slice the pulp finely. Add to the pan and mix well over low heat for 3 or 4 minutes.

■ Stir in the garam masala, cook for a minute and add in half the cilantro. Serve sprinkled with the remaining cilantro.

PALAK PANEER KASOORI

This is a wonderfully satisfying, substantial and tasty north Indian vegetarian dish. The paneer (Indian cheese) combines beautifully with the robust flavors of fenugreek.

SERVES 4–6

Preparation and cooking time: 30 minutes

3 tbsp olive oil
1 onion, sliced
1 tsp ground cumin
1-inch (2.5 cm) piece of ginger, grated
1 green chili, finely sliced
9 oz (250 g) shredded spinach

7 oz (200 g) fresh fenugreek leaves or 2 oz (50 g) dried fenugreek leaves, rinsed
7 fl oz (200 mL) curry sauce (page 32)
1 tsp salt
1 quantity of paneer (page 24)

- Heat 2 tablespoons of the oil in a deep, heavy-based frying pan, and fry the onion until starting to color. Stir in the cumin, ginger and green chili. Fry for a minute until aromatic.

- Add the spinach and fenugreek, and stir-fry on medium heat for 3 minutes. Add the curry sauce and salt, and bring to a boil. Turn down the heat and simmer for 15 minutes, stirring occasionally until all the liquid has evaporated.

- Meanwhile, heat the remainder of the oil in a separate frying pan and fry the paneer until golden brown on all sides.

- Add the paneer to the vegetables and cook for another 5 minutes, stirring often.

- Serve.

SHABNAM CURRY

This is another northern Indian dish contributed to Indian cuisine by the Mughals. It has a thick, dryish sauce and a mild, but delicious, flavor.

SERVES 4–6

Preparation and cooking time: 30 minutes

1 large or 2 small potatoes
3 tbsp olive oil
2 ripe tomatoes, chopped
1 tsp salt
1 tsp ground coriander
1/2 tsp turmeric
9 oz (250 g) button mushrooms, halved

4 oz (125 g) fresh or frozen peas
11 fl oz (300 mL) curry sauce (page 32)
1/2 tsp chili powder
2 tbsp cashew nuts, ground to a paste
1/2 tsp garam masala
1 tbsp chopped cilantro

■ Peel the potato and cut into 1-inch (2.5 cm) chunks. Cook in boiling salted water until just tender. Drain.

■ Meanwhile, heat the oil in a deep, heavy-based frying pan and add the tomatoes and salt. Stir-fry for 4–5 minutes until the tomatoes are pulpy and the oil has separated from the mixture.

■ Stir in the coriander and turmeric and fry for a minute. Add the mushrooms and peas and stir-fry on medium heat for 5 minutes.

■ Add the curry sauce, chili powder and potato and bring to a boil. Turn down the heat and simmer gently for 5 minutes, stirring now and then.

■ Stir in the cashew nut paste and garam masala, and simmer for another 5 minutes, stirring often.

■ Serve sprinkled with the cilantro.

Hatho Brinjal

Eggplant is a common and popular vegetable in Indian cooking. Easy to grow and nutritious, it is incredibly versatile. It can be fried, roasted, stuffed, mashed, pickled and anything in between!

Good on its own, it also marries well with potatoes as in this south Indian dish.

SERVES 4–6 Preparation and cooking time: 30 minutes	4 small eggplants (approx. 9 oz or 250 g) 1 large or 2 small potatoes 4 tbsp olive oil 1 tsp ground cumin 1 tsp ground coriander 2 ripe tomatoes, chopped 1 tsp salt	1 tsp turmeric 2 tbsp grated coconut (or shredded coconut) 13 fl oz (350 mL) curry sauce (page 32) 1 tsp chili powder 3 oz (100 g) frozen peas 1/2 tsp garam masala 1 tbsp chopped cilantro

■ Slice each eggplant in half and each half into 3 or 4 thick slices depending on the size of the eggplant. Peel the potatoes and cut into slices a little smaller than the eggplant.

■ Heat the oil in a deep, heavy-based frying pan, add the cumin and coriander and fry for a few seconds.

■ Stir in the tomatoes and salt and cook for 2–3 minutes, then add the turmeric and coconut. Stir-fry for a minute and add the potato and eggplant.

■ Stir-fry for about 3 minutes on medium heat and add the curry sauce and chili powder. Bring to a boil, cover and simmer for 15 minutes, stirring once or twice until the vegetables are tender. Add a little water if the sauce is becoming too dry.

■ Add the peas and simmer, uncovered, for another 5 minutes until the liquid has evaporated.

■ Stir in the garam masala and simmer for a minute. Serve sprinkled with cilantro.

TARKA DHAL

This easy-cook, one-pot recipe is a godsend when you need something quick and simple as a side dish. It goes well with any meat or vegetable curry and is also great with tandoori meats to make a complete meal.

Leaving the salt until the end helps the lentils cook a lot quicker.

SERVES 4	4 heaped tbsp good-quality red split lentils	1 ripe tomato, chopped
Preparation and cooking time: 35–40 minutes	15 fl oz (425 mL) water	1 green chili, finely chopped
	1 small onion, chopped	1 level tsp salt
	3 cloves of garlic, finely chopped	1/2 tsp garam masala
	2 tbsp olive oil	1 tbsp finely chopped cilantro
	1/4 tsp turmeric	

■ Rinse the lentils several times and place in a pan with all the other ingredients except the salt, garam masala and cilantro.

■ Bring to a boil and simmer, uncovered, for about 10 minutes, stirring now and then. Cover the pan and simmer for another 20 minutes, stirring two or three times. Add a little more water if the dhal looks too thick.

■ Stir in the salt, garam masala and half the cilantro. Serve sprinkled with the remaining cilantro.

17.   BIRYANIS

BIRYANI is to India what risotto is to Italy and the paella is to Spain, only more so. Among Indians there is an intense patriotism about this sumptuous dish; a sense of pride and splendor. In many parts of India, no lavish feast could lay claim to that status without the presence of biryani.

The true biryani is indeed a magnificent dish; the best basmati rice layered with succulent meats in delicious sauces, flavored with exquisite "sweet" spices such as saffron, cardamom, cinnamon, cloves and nutmeg, gently baked in sealed pots until the aromas and flavors permeate the layers and, finally, adorned with expensive ingredients like almonds, pistachios, cashews and dried fruits braised in pure ghee (clarified butter).

Its attraction is legendary. One tale has it that biryani was created by the beautiful Mumtaz Mahal, the queen of King Shah Jehan (the famous Taj Mahal was built by the king as her tomb after she died during childbirth), as a means of providing a complete meal to feed their army.

With such a lavish concoction, the princely Mughals inevitably played a significant part in the creation of the biryani. Food historians believe that the dish originated in Persia and was introduced to India by the extravagant, food-loving Mughals during the early part of the 16th century. Indeed, the word *biryani* is derived from the Persian word *birian*, which means "fried or roasted before cooking."

The popularity and importance of biryani quickly spread throughout the Middle East, South Asia and Southeast Asia, and an enormous variety of biryanis have been developed, many taking on the name of the region or the ruler of the time. So high was the status granted to this dish, there are claims that the earlier Punjabi *nawabs* (provincial governors or viceroys of regions during the Mughal era) wore a particular turban for each variety of biryani popular in the region.

Traditionally, goat meat was used to make biryani, but nowadays it is common to use lamb, chicken, fish and vegetables of all types. The common threads are the layers of cooked rice between the meat and vegetables, the sealed-pot (*dum*) style of cooking, and the unfading importance still attached to this fabulous dish.

PREPARATION FOR BIRYANIS

A good biryani should be spicy with lots of sweet and savory aromas, but never hot. Traditional biryanis, like many other traditional Indian dishes, incorporate a dozen or more spices and take hours of preparation and cooking, with each variety of biryani differing in the combination of spices used according to the style of cooking of the region.

Restaurant methods simplify the process by the prior preparation of meat, sauces and basic spice blends, adding specific ingredients as required for a particular recipe. You can use chicken as prepared for chicken curries (page 59) or lamb as prepared for lamb curries (page 71).

You will also need to prepare a small quantity of the following Biryani Spice Blend.

Biryani Spice Blend

1 tsp green cardamom pods
1 tsp cloves
1 tsp fennel seeds
1 tsp mace
2 tsp cumin seeds
two 1-inch (2.5 cm) sticks of cinnamon
1 nutmeg, crushed

Grind all the ingredients to a fine powder in an electric grinder or pestle and mortar. Place in a small jar, label and store in a cool, dark place for no more than 6 weeks for best results.

Accompaniments to Biryani

A good biryani is full of flavor and aroma, but it is quite a dry dish. Traditionally it is served with yogurt, pickles, spicy salads and chutneys, and does not require a sauce or gravy. However, restaurant biryanis generally come with a curry sauce on the side to satisfy the Western penchant for sauce. I have included recipes for traditional and modern accompaniments to the biryani.

Ulli Surka (onion and chili salad)

1 red onion, sliced
2 green chilies, deseeded and sliced
3 tbsp water
1/2 tsp salt flakes

Combine all the ingredients in a small bowl, crushing the chilies with the back of a spoon to release the flavors. Allow to stand for about 30 minutes before serving.

BIRYANI CHAMMANTHI

6 tbsp grated fresh coconut
2 green chilies, coarsely chopped
2 tsp grated ginger
handful of mint leaves
handful of cilantro
4 fl oz (120 mL) yogurt
$\frac{1}{2}$ tsp salt

Grind the coconut, chilies, ginger, mint and cilantro to a coarse paste. Combine with the yogurt and salt.

YOGURT CHUTNEY

9 fl oz (250 mL) plain yogurt
6 tbsp shredded cilantro
3 tbsp shredded mint leaves
2 green chilies, finely sliced
1 clove of garlic, finely sliced
$\frac{1}{2}$ tsp green mango powder
$\frac{1}{2}$ tsp salt

Combine all the ingredients in a small bowl. Allow to stand for 30 minutes before serving.

CURRY SAUCE

18 fl oz/1 US pint (500 mL) curry sauce (page 32)
1 tsp chili powder
$\frac{1}{2}$ tsp paprika
$\frac{1}{2}$ tsp salt
$\frac{1}{2}$ tsp garam masala

In a clean pan, bring the curry sauce to a boil and simmer for 5 minutes until slightly thickened. Stir in the remaining ingredients. Simmer for a minute and serve.

Biryani dishes

Malabar Shrimp Biryani
Gentle spice aromas with succulent shrimp.

Kozhikode Chicken Biryani
Chicken pieces with fresh herbs and aromatic spices.

Shahi Biryani
A sumptuous lamb dish cooked in the lavish style of the grand Mughal emperors.

Hyderabadi Vegetable Biryani
A vegetarian dish that combines the rich, creamy style of north Indian cuisine and the pungent, sharp flavors of the south.

MALABAR SHRIMP BIRYANI

Malabar is a region of southern India nestling along the southwest coast of the Indian peninsula. Its cuisine is generally milder and gentler than that of its immediate neighbors. The Malabar region is synonymous with biryani, and seafood, such as the shrimp in this recipe, is a common ingredient in many of its dishes.

SERVES 4 Preparation and cooking time: 35 minutes	4 tbsp olive oil 1 onion, sliced 4 bay leaves, fresh or dried 1 tsp biryani spice blend (page 144) 1 green chili, finely sliced 1 lb (450 g) raw shrimp 11 fl oz (300 mL) curry sauce (page 32)	3 fl oz (100 mL) coconut milk 2 tsp lemon juice 1 tsp salt 1 lb 12 oz (800 g) saffron pilau rice (page 166) 1 tbsp grated coconut 1 tbsp chopped cilantro

■ Preheat the oven to 400°F (200°C).

■ Heat the oil in a deep, heavy-based frying pan and add the onion. Fry on medium heat for about 3 minutes until translucent.

■ Add the bay leaves, spice blend and chili, and fry for another minute. Stir in the shrimp and stir-fry for 2 minutes.

■ Add the curry sauce, coconut milk, lemon juice and salt. Bring to a boil and simmer for 5 minutes.

■ Meanwhile, microwave the rice on high for 2 minutes. Fluff up the rice gently with a fork and place half in a deep ovenproof dish with a tight-fitting lid.

■ Spoon the shrimp mixture over the rice layer and cover with the remaining rice. Put the lid firmly on the dish and place in the oven for 20 minutes.

■ Serve sprinkled with the grated coconut and cilantro, and with accompaniments of choice.

Kozhikode Chicken Biryani

Kozhikode is a city in the southern Indian coastal state of Kerala. Its cuisine has been described as one of the world's earliest fusion cuisines with influences from the Tamils, Arabs, East Asians, Sinhalese and even the Mughals.

Kozhikode is famous for its biryanis, typically served with vinegary pickles and popadoms.

SERVES 4

Preparation and cooking time: 35 minutes

- 3 tbsp olive oil
- 6 curry leaves, fresh or frozen
- 2 cloves of garlic, finely chopped
- 1-inch (2.5 cm) piece of ginger, finely chopped (or a portion of prepared garlic-and-ginger mix, page 30, thawed)
- 2 green chilies, finely chopped (or half a portion of prepared chilies, page 30)
- 1/2 tsp turmeric
- 1 tsp biryani spice blend (page 144)
- 1 tsp poppy seeds, ground to a paste
- 15 fl oz (425 mL) curry sauce (page 32)
- 1/2 tsp salt
- 1 lb (450 g) precooked chicken (page 59)
- 7 fl oz (200 mL) plain yogurt
- 2 tbsp chopped cilantro
- 2 tbsp chopped mint leaves
- 1 tbsp lime juice
- 1 lb 12 oz (800 g) pilau rice (page 163)
- 2 tbsp melted ghee (clarified butter, page 24)
- 1 tbsp raw cashew nuts
- 1 tbsp sultana raisins
- 1 hard-boiled egg, sliced

- Preheat the oven to 400°F (200°C).

- Heat the oil in a deep, heavy-based frying pan and add the curry leaves, garlic, ginger and chilies. Fry for a minute or two on medium heat and add the turmeric, spice blend and poppy-seed paste. Cook for another minute.

- Stir in the curry sauce and salt and bring to a boil. Boil for 5 minutes, then add the chicken and yogurt.

- Bring back to a boil and simmer for 3 minutes. Turn off the heat and stir in the cilantro, mint and lime juice.

- Meanwhile, microwave the rice on high for 2 minutes. Fluff up the rice gently with a fork and place half in a deep ovenproof dish with a tight-fitting lid.

- Spoon the chicken mixture over the rice layer and cover with the remaining rice. Put the lid firmly on the dish and place in the oven for 20 minutes.

- Heat the ghee in a small pan and gently braise the cashew nuts and raisins until the nuts turn a pale golden brown and the raisins plump up.

- Serve the biryani garnished with the egg slices and sprinkled with the nuts and raisins.

SHAHI BIRYANI

Mughlai cuisine, so named because it originates from the era of the grand Mughals, is renowned for being rich and lavish. Among the many and varied cuisines that were to become native to India, this one has been at the forefront of shaping the way Indians cook and eat today. This delicious dish is testament to that magnificent era.

SERVES 4	4 tbsp melted ghee (clarified butter, page 24)	15 fl oz (425 mL) curry sauce (page 32)
Preparation and cooking time: 45 minutes	2 tbsp almonds, blanched	1/2 tsp chili powder
	2 tbsp golden raisins	1/2 tsp salt
	1 tsp saffron	1 lb (450 g) precooked lamb (page 71)
	4 tbsp milk, warmed	3 fl oz (100 mL) plain yogurt
	3 tbsp olive oil	3 fl oz (100 mL) light cream
	1 onion, sliced	1/2 tsp garam masala
	2 cloves of garlic, finely sliced	1 tbsp chopped cilantro
	1 1/2 tsp biryani spice blend (page 144)	1 lb 12 oz (800 g) saffron pilau rice (page 166)

- Preheat the oven to 400°F (200°C).

- Heat the ghee in a small pan and gently braise the almonds and raisins until the nuts have turned a pale golden brown, and the raisins have plumped up. Set aside.

- Add the saffron to the warmed milk, stir and set aside.

- Heat the oil in a deep, heavy-based frying pan and add the onion. Stir-fry on medium heat until crisp. Remove with a slotted spoon and set aside.

- Add the garlic to the oil remaining in the pan and stir-fry for a few seconds. Stir in the spice blend and cook for another few seconds until aromatic.

- Add the curry sauce, chili powder and salt, and bring to a boil. Cook on high heat for 5 minutes until the sauce is thick.

- Stir in the lamb and yogurt, and bring back to a boil. Simmer for 5 minutes, then stir in the cream. Bring back to a gentle simmer and simmer for another 5 minutes before stirring in the garam masala and cilantro.

- Meanwhile, microwave the rice on high for 2 minutes. Fluff up the rice gently with a fork and place half in a deep ovenproof dish with a tight-fitting lid. Sprinkle half the onion, almonds, raisins, melted ghee and saffron milk over the rice.

- Spoon the lamb mixture over the rice layer and cover with the remaining rice. Sprinkle the remaining onion, almonds, raisins, melted ghee and saffron milk over the rice.

- Put the lid firmly on the dish and place in the oven for 20 minutes. Serve with accompaniments of choice.

HYDERABADI VEGETABLE BIRYANI

Another famous biryani created from a melding of the rich, creamy aromatic dishes of northern India and the sharp, piquant and pungent flavors of the south.

SERVES 4

Preparation and cooking time: 45 minutes

6 tbsp light cream, warmed
1 tsp saffron
4 tbsp ghee (clarified butter, page 24) or olive oil
3 green chilies, finely chopped
   (or half a portion of prepared chilies, page 30)
1/2 tsp turmeric
1 tsp biryani spice blend (page 144)
1 large potato, peeled and diced
3 carrots, peeled and diced
1 tbsp almonds, blanched

1 tbsp cashew nuts
1 tbsp sultana raisins
14 fl oz (400 mL) curry sauce (page 32)
1 tsp salt
1/2 tsp chili powder
3 fl oz (100 mL) plain yogurt
2 tbsp chopped mint
2 tbsp chopped cilantro
1 lime, juiced
1 lb 12 oz (800 g) pilau rice (page 163)

■ Combine the warm cream and saffron, and set aside.

■ Heat the ghee or oil in a deep, heavy-based frying pan and add the chilies, turmeric and spice blend. Stir for a few seconds and add the vegetables.

■ Stir-fry on gentle heat for 3 minutes and add the nuts, raisins, curry sauce, salt and chili powder. Bring to a boil, cover and simmer for 10–15 minutes until the vegetables are just tender.

■ Stir in the yogurt and half the saffron cream, and simmer for another 5 minutes before stirring in the mint and cilantro.

■ Meanwhile, microwave the rice on high for 2 minutes. Fluff up the rice gently with a fork and place half in a deep ovenproof dish with a tight-fitting lid. Sprinkle half the lime juice over the mixture.

■ Spoon the vegetable mixture over the rice layer and cover with the remaining rice. Sprinkle the remaining lime juice and saffron cream over the dish.

■ Put the lid firmly on the dish and place in the oven for 20 minutes. Serve hot with accompaniments of choice.

18.   BREADS

B READ OF SOME type or another, referred to as *roti*, is essential for a complete meal for most Indians. Wheat has been cultivated on the Indian subcontinent for over 8,000 years and the majority of Indian bread is made from wheat flour. However, maize, corn, lentils and rice are all used in some shape or form to make different kinds of roti. Methods of cooking roti vary according to the type and the region, but can be broadly divided into three main cooking styles, the most common of which uses a hot griddle (*tava*). The dough is prepared from wheat flour and water and expertly rolled out to a thin round before being slapped onto the preheated tava. The roti is quickly turned to cook the other side, turned again and slipped onto the hot coals for a few seconds to puff it up.

Another cooking style that is quite popular throughout India is frying, either "shallow" frying in butter or ghee as for parathas, or deep-frying in ghee or oil as for pooris and bhatooras. Parathas are flat breads that are layered with ghee and shallow-fried on a tava. Sometimes, cooked spicy lentils, grated vegetables or chopped fenugreek is added to the dough. For other variations, cooked, spiced potato, cauliflower or a mixture of vegetables is used to "stuff" the paratha before rolling. Pooris and bhatooras, sometimes flavored with carom, cumin or poppy seeds, are golden, deep-fried, puffy rounds of dough often served at festive occasions.

Tandoori roti and naan, a particularly popular type of flat bread in the West, are oven-baked using an electric or traditional charcoal-fired tandoor. The dough for the naan is leavened using yeast, yogurt cultures or baking powder before being baked.

COOKING INDIAN BREADS AT HOME

Naan, plain and flavored, is the most popular type of bread on the Indian restaurant menu, but the other varieties are well worth a try. The tandoor is without doubt the best way of cooking naan, but I have found that with a few modifications you can get really good results at home with a large tava or frying pan and a good grill.

Heat your frying pan or tava, and cook your naan for about 2 minutes each side, turning once or twice. It will puff up beautifully. Alternatively, cook one side on the tava or frying pan and place under a grill to cook the upper side — you will need to do this anyway if you are putting ingredients onto one side of the naan.

Brush the cooked naan with extra-virgin olive oil or butter and keep warm in a clean tea towel while cooking the remainder.

BREADS

PLAIN NAAN
Leavened flat bread, deliciously light, puffy and soft, brushed with extra-virgin olive oil.

GARLIC NAAN
Leavened flat bread, sprinkled with finely chopped fresh garlic.

PESHWARI NAAN
Leavened flat bread, stuffed with toasted nuts and dried fruit.

MIRCHI NAAN
Leavened flat bread, sprinkled with marinated onions and sliced green chilies.

STUFFED PARATHA
Unleavened whole-wheat flat bread, layered with butter, stuffed with spicy potatoes and panfried with extra-virgin olive oil until crispy.

POORI
Unleavened whole-wheat flat bread, deepfried until puffed and golden.

BASIC NAAN RECIPE

This is a really simple recipe but it produces wonderful results. If you have a bread maker, use it on the dough setting, but only let it knead for about 5 minutes. Dough that's kneaded long enough to make good bread loaves becomes too elastic to roll out easily to make naan. You can leave the dough to rise in the bread pan with the machine switched off.

MAKES 6 NAAN Preparation time: 10 minutes plus about an hour to let the dough rise	approx. 11 fl oz (300 mL) water 2 tsp sugar 3 tsp instant dried yeast	1 tbsp oil 1 lb (450 g) white bread flour or plain white flour 1 tsp salt

- Warm the water slightly, pour into a large bowl and add the sugar, yeast and oil.

- Add the flour and sprinkle the salt over the flour. Using your hand, mix and bring the ingredients together, adding more water or more flour until you have a soft but non-sticky dough.

- Place the dough onto a clean, lightly floured surface and knead it for 5 minutes until smooth.

- Put the dough in a lightly greased bowl, cover with a damp tea towel or greased cling wrap. Stand the bowl in a draft-free place for about an hour or until the dough has doubled in size.

- Degas the dough by punching it down and knead briefly before using.

- The dough can be kept in the fridge for up to 2 days. It will rise quite quickly at first until it cools down, so check it frequently and punch it down.

Freezing: The dough can be frozen for up to a month.

TIP

If you are planning to make several naan, have sheets of parchment paper or thick paper towels handy. Roll out your naan, place on a sheet of paper and place another sheet of paper on top. Repeat with up to 6 naan; any more and you might find the bottom ones stick. Cook as soon as possible.

PLAIN NAAN

MAKES 6 NAAN	1 quantity of basic naan dough (page 153)
Preparation and cooking time: 20 minutes	1 tbsp extra-virgin olive oil

- Divide the dough into 6 portions.

- Roll a portion into a thin round or teardrop shape and cook on a hot tava or frying pan for about 2 minutes on each side until it is puffed and brown spots start to appear.

- Alternatively, cook the underside on the tava and place under a very hot grill for about a minute to cook the top.

- Wrap in a clean tea towel to keep warm while cooking the remaining naan.

- Brush with the oil and serve.

GARLIC NAAN

MAKES 6 NAAN Preparation and cooking time: 20 minutes	1 quantity of basic naan dough (page 153) 1 tbsp extra-virgin olive oil 3 cloves of garlic, finely chopped

■ Divide the dough into 6 portions.

■ Roll a portion into a thin round or teardrop shape, brush with the oil and sprinkle with the garlic. Press the garlic down into the dough very lightly.

■ Cook the naan on a hot tava or frying pan for about 2 minutes and place under a very hot grill for a another minute or so.

■ Wrap in a clean tea towel to keep warm while cooking the remaining naan.

PESHWARI NAAN

MAKES 6 NAAN	2 tbsp almonds, blanched	1 quantity of basic naan dough (page 153)
	2 tbsp pistachios	1 tbsp sliced almonds
Preparation and	2 tbsp raisins	1 tbsp extra-virgin olive oil
cooking time:	2 tsp finely granulated sugar	
30 minutes		

- Roast the nuts in a hot pan on gentle heat until the almonds start to color. Cool.

- Chop the nuts and raisins finely, or process briefly in a food processor and combine with the sugar. Set aside.

- Divide the dough into 6 portions. Roll one portion into a thick round and place about 1 tablespoon of the nut-and-raisin mixture onto one half of the round, about 1 inch (2.5 cm) from the edge.

- Dampen the edges slightly with water and bring the other half over the mixture and press to seal the edges.

- Carefully roll out the naan, stretching it to form a teardrop shape. Sprinkle with flaked almonds, pressing them down into the dough lightly.

- Cook the naan on a hot tava or frying pan for about 2 minutes and place under a very hot grill for a another minute or so.

- Wrap in a clean tea towel to keep warm while cooking the remaining naan.

- Brush with olive oil and serve hot.

MIRCHI NAAN

MAKES 6 NAAN	1 onion, finely sliced	1/2 tsp ground coriander
Preparation and cooking time: 40 minutes	1/2 tsp salt 2 green chilies, deseeded and finely sliced 1/2 tsp ground cumin	1 quantity of basic naan dough (page 153) 1 tbsp extra-virgin olive oil

■ Combine the onion and salt in a small bowl and allow to stand for about 20 minutes. Drain off any liquid and mix in the chilies, cumin and coriander.

■ Divide the dough into 6 portions.

■ Roll a portion into a thin round or teardrop shape, brush with oil and sprinkle with the onion-and-chili mixture, pressing it down into the dough very lightly.

■ Cook the naan on a hot tava or frying pan for about 2 minutes and place under a very hot grill for another minute or so. Brush with more olive oil.

■ Wrap in a clean tea towel to keep warm while cooking the remaining naan.

STUFFED PARATHA

These delicious breads are a meal in themselves but they can also be served with dhals and curries for a substantial accompaniment.

MAKES 4 PARATHA	8 oz (225 g) chapati flour, plus extra for dusting	½ tsp turmeric
Preparation and cooking time: 30 minutes	4 fl oz (110 mL) water 1 large potato, grated 1 tsp salt 1 tsp garam masala	2 green chilies, finely chopped, or 1 tsp chili powder 2 oz (50 g) butter, softened 4 tbsp extra-virgin olive oil

■ Place the flour in a large mixing bowl and slowly add the water, mixing the flour and water together until you have a soft, pliable dough.

■ Using damp hands, knead the dough briefly, fold into a neat shape, cover and set aside for 10–15 minutes.

■ Squeeze excess liquid out of the potato and combine with the salt, garam masala, turmeric and chilies.

■ Heat a tava or heavy-based frying pan on low to medium heat. Take two golf-ball-sized pieces of dough and, using the extra flour for dusting, roll both out to about the size of a saucer.

■ Spread a little butter on one round of dough to about 1 inch (2.5 cm) from the edge and cover with about 1 tablespoon of the potato filling.

■ Place the second round of dough over the potato filling and press to seal the edges. Dust with flour and roll out to about the size of a dinner plate.

■ Slap the paratha from one hand to the other to remove any excess flour, which will burn if left on.

■ Place onto a medium-hot tava and brush or spray olive oil onto the upper side. Flip over and brush or spray the other side with oil.

■ Cook for about 30 seconds and flip over and brush with a little more oil. Repeat the process after another 30 seconds or so.

■ If the tava or pan is at the right heat, the paratha should take about 3 minutes to cook. When cooked, the paratha will be crisp at the edges and a nice golden brown with large dark-brown spots. If those spots are black, the heat is too high; if they are not brown enough, the heat is not high enough.

■ Wrap the paratha loosely in foil to keep it warm while making the remaining parathas. Serve hot with pickles and spiced yogurt.

TIP

For a variation, boil and mash the potato instead of grating it. Allow it to cool, mix with the spices and proceed as above.

POORI

These deep-fried little breads are often made with plain white flour, but I think whole-wheat chapati flour gives them a better flavor. Pooris are a good choice if you are planning to serve a large number of people as they are quick to prepare and reheat well.

MAKES 18–20 POORI	1 lb (450 g) chapati flour, plus extra for dusting
Preparation and cooking time: 30 minutes	1 tsp salt 8 fl oz (220 mL) water oil for deep-frying

■ Place the flour in a large mixing bowl, sprinkle with the salt and slowly add the water, mixing the flour and water together until you have a soft, pliable dough.

■ Using damp hands, knead the dough briefly, fold into a neat shape, cover and set aside for 10–15 minutes.

■ Fill a karahi or deep saucepan about two-thirds full of oil and heat the oil until it is hot but not smoking.

■ Take a piece of dough about the size of a golf ball and roll into a round about 6 inches (15 cm) in diameter and very thin (about ⅟₂₅ of an inch or 1 mm thick). Repeat with 3–5 more pieces of dough depending on the size of your karahi.

■ Quickly slide the pooris into the hot oil. They should rise to the surface within about 6 seconds and begin to puff up. As they do, gently flip them over for a few seconds to lightly brown the other side. The whole process should take about 15 seconds.

■ Remove the pooris and drain them on a wire rack placed over a tray. Repeat with the remaining dough.

■ Serve immediately or wrap in foil. Reheat for a few seconds in the microwave or place on a baking tray, cover with foil and put in a hot oven for about 15 minutes.

19. Rice dishes

THERE IS SOME speculation about the origins of rice but it appears to have a long history going back to 3000 BCE when, it is believed, Indian natives discovered the rice plant growing in the wild and began experimenting with it. Today, rice is grown and harvested on every continent with the exception of Antarctica, where growing conditions are completely unsuitable.

Two-thirds of the world's population relies on rice as a food source. Rice is the staple food of 65 percent of the Indian population and in more recent times has become the principal crop grown in the country. Rice cultivation is carried out in all Indian states — many would say to the detriment of the environment due to the crop's high water requirement — and India now ranks second only to China in world rice production. Rice-based industries are a source of employment and income for more than 50 million households within India.

Although about 600 new varieties of rice have been developed during the last 30 years, basmati rice remains the most prized. The basmati grain is slender and aromatic with a nutty flavor and superior cooking qualities for a light, fluffy, flavorful result.

PILAU RICE DISHES

Here are a few simple tips to help make rice cooking a breeze:

• Always measure the rice and water carefully to ensure that you get a perfect result with the rice grains firm and separate, and not soft and soggy. One measure of rice to one-and-a-half measures of water is the perfect proportion for savory basmati rice dishes.

• Drain the rice well after washing it to ensure it is quite dry before cooking (some cooks say rice should never be washed, but I prefer to wash it).

• Always cook the rice well in oil or ghee as directed. This cooks the outer layer of starch and helps keep the grains separate.

• Once the water is boiling, keep the heat as low as possible and ensure the pot is well sealed with a tight-fitting lid. "Dry" the rice in a warm oven for a few minutes if possible.

• Gently fluff up the rice before serving.

Rice is versatile, nutritious, healthy, nonallergenic and gluten free. It is naturally low in fat, cholesterol and sodium, and has only 200 calories per cup cooked. Products such as alcoholic liquor (*sake*), glue and even clothing are made from rice or rice products in the rice-producing regions throughout the world.

It is no wonder, then, that the grain is regarded with such reverence within many cultures that it is used for religious offerings, and to throw leftover rice away is considered sinful. To add to its virtues, uncooked white rice can be kept indefinitely as long as it is kept dry, and uncooked basmati rice actually improves with age.

To prevent any bacteria in the rice from causing food poisoning, it's best to serve rice when it has just been cooked. However, if that is not possible, you should cool the rice as quickly as possible (ideally within one hour) and keep it in the fridge for no more than one day until reheating. Reheated rice should be piping hot and rice should not be reheated more than once.

Rice dishes

Pilau Rice
Basmati rice flavored with whole spices and ghee.

Egg Fried Rice
Basmati rice with fried egg.

Peshwari Pilau
Basmati rice with almonds, pistachios and dried fruit.

Saffron Pilau
Basmati rice delicately flavored with saffron and cardamom.

Mushroom Pilau
Basmati rice with mushroom.

PILAU RICE

Colorful and beautifully aromatic, this is still the most popular rice dish on the menu. Its appearance, however, relies on artificial food colorings. If you don't like the idea of that, leave them out; they don't contribute to the flavor.

SERVES 4

Preparation and cooking time: about 30 minutes

9 oz (250 g) basmati rice
1/2 tsp yellow food coloring
1/2 tsp red food coloring
1 tbsp ghee (clarified butter, page 24) or olive oil
2 tsp finely chopped onion
6 green cardamoms

two 1-inch (2.5 cm) sticks of cinnamon
4 cloves
2 bay leaves
15 fl oz (425 mL) cold water
1/2 tsp salt

- Wash the rice several times and leave to drain in a large sieve.

- If you are using it, mix each food coloring with about a tablespoon of water, keeping the two colors separate, and set aside.

- Preheat the oven to 325°F (170°C).

- Meanwhile, heat the ghee or oil in a heavy-based pan with a tight-fitting lid, and fry the onion until just translucent.

- Add the cardamoms, cinnamon, cloves and bay leaves, and cook for 1 minute.

- Add the drained rice and mix well to coat all the grains with the ghee or oil. Cook on medium heat for about a minute.

- Stir in the water and salt, and bring to a boil. Once boiling, turn the heat to very low and place the lid on the pan.

- Stir the rice after about 5 minutes, and again after 3 minutes. Re-cover and leave for another 4–5 minutes, after which time all the water will have been absorbed.

- Add the food colorings to the rice, if you are using them, by spooning in two separate lines across the rice for each color.

- Replace the lid and put the pan in the oven for about 20 minutes to dry off the rice and set the colors.

- Transfer the pilau to a serving dish, taking care not to break the grains of rice. Fluff up with a fork. Serve immediately or cool as quickly as possible and refrigerate for use the next day.

- Reheat in a microwave oven for about 2 minutes.

EGG FRIED RICE

This is quite a substantial dish to serve on its own, but is particularly so when combined with some precooked vegetables or when eaten with a dhal.

SERVES 4	9 oz (250 g) basmati rice	1 tsp salt
Preparation and cooking time: 30 minutes	6 green cardamoms 1-inch (2.5 cm) stick of cinnamon 4 cloves 2 bay leaves	2 tbsp ghee (clarified butter, page 24) or olive oil 2 tsp finely chopped onion 2 eggs, lightly beaten 2 tbsp soy sauce

■ Wash the rice several times in cold water and add to a large pan with the whole spices.

■ Add plenty of cold water so that the water is 3 or 4 inches (7–10 cm) above the rice and bring to a boil.

■ Stir in the salt and simmer for about 12 minutes or until the rice is cooked. Drain through a large sieve.

■ Place the sieve over a pan or bowl and leave the rice to drain completely. Remove the whole spices if preferred.

■ Meanwhile, heat half the ghee or oil in a heavy-based frying pan and fry the onion for about a minute.

■ Add the beaten egg and tilt the pan to spread the egg accross the base of the pan. Cook over medium heat for about 3 minutes until it is completely set.

■ Remove the omelette from the pan, roll up tightly and slice the roll thinly to obtain strips of omelette.

■ Heat the remaining ghee or oil in a karahi or large pan and add the drained rice. Stir-fry over medium heat for 4–5 minutes until heated through.

■ Sprinkle the soy sauce on top and add the omelette pieces. Stir-fry for another minute and serve.

PESHWARI PILAU

The nuts and sultana raisins, lightly roasted in ghee, add a lovely crunch and sweetness to this rice dish. It is great with spicy curries.

SERVES 4	9 oz (250 g) basmati rice	6 green cardamoms
	2 tbsp almonds, blanched	6 cloves
Preparation and cooking time: 30 minutes	2 tbsp pistachios	two 1-inch (2.5 cm) sticks of cinnamon
	1 tbsp ghee (clarified butter, page 24) or olive oil	15 fl oz (425 mL) cold water
	2 tbsp sultana raisins or golden raisins	1/2 tsp salt

■ Wash the rice several times and leave to drain in a large sieve. Chop the almonds and pistachios coarsely.

■ Preheat the oven to 325°F (170°C).

■ Heat the ghee or oil in a heavy-based pan with a tight-fitting lid and add the nuts, raisins and whole spices. Cook gently for about 2 minutes, stirring.

■ Add the drained rice and mix well to coat all the grains with the ghee or oil. Cook on medium heat for about a minute.

■ Stir in the water and salt, and bring to a boil. Once boiling, turn the heat to very low and place the lid on the pan.

■ Stir the rice after about 5 minutes, and again after 3 minutes. Re-cover and leave for another 4–5 minutes, after which time all the water will have been absorbed.

■ Place the pan in the oven for about 20 minutes to dry off the rice.

■ Transfer the pilau to a serving dish, taking care not to break the grains of rice. Fluff up with a fork. Serve immediately or cool as quickly as possible and refrigerate for use the next day.

■ Reheat in a microwave oven for about 2 minutes.

SAFFRON PILAU

Saffron is an expensive spice with a sweet, delicate aroma and deep auburn color. It needs to be soaked in warm milk for a few minutes to release its color and aroma. The resulting dish will be a pale yellow color.

SERVES 4

Preparation and cooking time: 30 minutes

1 tsp saffron strands
3 tbsp warm milk
9 oz (250 g) basmati rice
1 tbsp ghee (clarified butter, page 24) or olive oil
2 tsp finely chopped onion

6 green cardamoms
2 bay leaves
15 fl oz (425 mL) cold water
1/2 tsp salt

■ Combine the saffron and warm milk and set aside. Meanwhile, preheat the oven to 325°F (170°C).

■ Wash the rice several times and leave to drain in a large sieve.

■ Heat the ghee or oil in a heavy-based pan with a tight-fitting lid, and fry the onion until just translucent. Add the cardamoms and bay leaves, and cook for 1 minute.

■ Add the drained rice and mix well to coat all the grains with the ghee or oil. Cook on medium heat for about a minute.

■ Stir in the water, saffron mixture and salt, and bring to a boil. Once boiling, turn the heat to very low and place the lid on the pan.

■ Stir the rice after about 5 minutes, and again after 3 minutes. Re-cover and leave for another 4–5 minutes, after which time all the water will have been absorbed.

■ Place the pan in the oven for about 20 minutes to dry off the rice.

■ Transfer the pilau to a serving dish, taking care not to break the grains of rice. Fluff up with a fork. Serve immediately or cool as quickly as possible and refrigerate for use the next day.

■ Reheat in a microwave oven for about 2 minutes.

TIP

For a "cheat's" version, use about 1/4 teaspoon of turmeric instead of the saffron. Stir in with the water.

Mushroom Pilau

This mildly spicy rice dish with the meaty texture and taste of mushrooms is a delicious accompaniment to meat curries.

SERVES 4

Preparation and cooking time: 30 minutes

9 oz (250 g) basmati rice
3 oz (100 g) button mushrooms
1 tbsp ghee (clarified butter, page 24) or olive oil
2 tbsp finely chopped onion
6 green cardamoms
6 cloves

two 1-inch (2.5 cm) sticks of cinnamon
2 bay leaves
1 tsp cracked black pepper
13 fl oz (375 mL) cold water
1/2 tsp salt
1/2 tsp turmeric

- Wash the rice several times and leave to drain in a large sieve. Preheat the oven to 325°F (170°C).

- Wipe the mushrooms, trim the stalks, and quarter. Heat the ghee or oil in a heavy-based pan with a tight-fitting lid and stir-fry the mushrooms for about 2 minutes until lightly browned.

- Add the onion and all the spices and stir-fry for another minute. Stir in the drained rice and mix well to coat all the grains with the ghee or oil. Cook on medium heat for about a minute.

- Add the water, salt and turmeric and bring to a boil. Once boiling, turn the heat to very low and place the lid on the pan.

- Stir the rice and mushrooms after about 5 minutes, and again after 3 minutes. Re-cover and leave for another 4–5 minutes, after which time all the water will have been absorbed.

- Place the pan in the oven for about 20 minutes to dry off the rice.

- Transfer the pilau to a serving dish, taking care not to break the grains of rice. Fluff up with a fork. Serve immediately or cool as quickly as possible and refrigerate for use the next day.

- Reheat in a microwave oven for about 2 minutes.

20.

ACCOMPANIMENTS
CHUTNEYS, PICKLES AND RAITA

RELISHLIKE condiments (*achaar*) and chutneys are embedded in Indian culture. In keeping with the richness and diversity of the cuisine, Indian pickles, chutneys and achaars, served with virtually every meal, come in a mind-boggling variety of types, flavors and colors. Mangoes, peaches, tomatoes, chilies, ginger, garlic, lemons, limes, carrots, eggplants, turnips, cauliflower, cilantro, mint, coconut and many more fruits and vegetables are turned into pickles and chutneys or used in spicy yogurt dishes such as raita. Some accompaniments are as simple as grinding or mixing ingredients together, while others are complex, time-consuming concoctions of dozens of spicy and exotic ingredients, matured over months.

Indian chutneys and pickles are packed with fresh or pungent spicy flavors and are served in small quantities to whet the appetite and enhance the meal.

Author's note: In order to prevent contamination and lengthen the shelf life of pickles and chutneys, it is necessary to sterilize storage jars, bottles and lids. This may be done by washing the jars and lids in very hot, soapy water and after draining, placing them in a moderately warm (300°F/150°C) oven for about 30 minutes. Use the jars straight out of the oven and fill them almost to the rim with hot chutney. Turn the jars upside down for two minutes to help seal them. I find wearing rubber gloves to handle the hot jars makes this task easier.

ACCOMPANIMENTS

MANGO CHUTNEY
A sweet chutney made with ripe mangoes.

PEACH CHUTNEY
A sweet, fruity chutney made with ripe peaches and raisins.

COCONUT AND MINT CHUTNEY
A tart, spicy chutney made with coconut, fresh mint and spices.

LEMON PICKLE
A tart, salty pickle made with quartered lemons.

CRUNCHY PICKLED VEGETABLES
A spicy, vinegary salad of mixed shredded vegetables.

MANGO PICKLE
A salty pickle of tart green mangoes and whole spices in oil.

RAITA
A spiced, yet cooling yogurt dish with a variety of shredded vegetables.

MANGO CHUTNEY

Sweet mango chutney is a popular accompaniment to spicy dishes. Good-quality mango chutney is quite expensive to buy so making your own not only saves you money, but you will find it tastes much better too.

This chutney will keep well for up to two years so you can make a large quantity when mangoes are cheap and plentiful.

MAKES ABOUT 28 FL OZ (800 ML)	4 lb 8 oz (2 kg) ripe mangoes
	18 fl oz/1 US pint (500 mL) white wine or cider vinegar
Preparation and cooking time: 1¹/₂ hours	13 oz (350 g) white sugar
	2 tsp grated ginger
	2 red chilies, deseeded and finely sliced (optional)

■ Peel the mangoes and discard the peel. Slice the flesh from the stones, chop coarsely and place in a large, heavy-based saucepan with all the remaining ingredients. Bring slowly to a boil, stirring to dissolve the sugar.

■ Simmer, partly covered, for 1 hour, stirring occasionally. Meanwhile, wash the jars and lids in hot soapy water, rinse well and dry in a warm oven. Please see the author's note about this on page 169.

■ Spoon the hot chutney carefully into the warm, clean jars, place the lids on firmly and invert each jar for two minutes.

■ Store the chutney in a cool, dry place. After opening, store in the fridge.

PEACH CHUTNEY

This sweet-and-sour, fruity chutney is a nice change from mango chutney and goes well with cold meats, cheese and sausages, as well as spicy curries. You can buy bruised and misshapen fruit but it's important that it is sweet and ripe, as tasteless fruit will produce a poor-quality chutney.

Ripe nectarines may be used instead of peaches.

MAKES ABOUT
18 FL OZ/1 US PINT
(500 ML)

Preparation and
cooking time:
2 hours

2 lb 4 oz (1 kg) ripe peaches
7 oz (200 g) golden raisins
9 fl oz (250 mL) cold water
2 large onions, sliced

13 fl oz (370 mL) malt vinegar
9 oz (250 g) white sugar
2 tsp grated ginger
1 tsp chili powder

■ Wash the fruit well, remove the stones and chop the flesh coarsely. Place in a large, heavy-based saucepan with the raisins and water, bring to a boil and simmer uncovered for 20 minutes, stirring once or twice.

■ Add all the remaining ingredients and bring slowly back to a boil, stirring to dissolve the sugar.

■ Simmer, partly covered, for about 1 hour and 15 minutes, stirring occasionally. Meanwhile, wash the jars and lids in hot soapy water, rinse well and dry in a warm oven. Please see the author's note about this on page 169.

■ Spoon the hot chutney carefully into the warm, clean jars, place the lids on firmly and invert each jar for two minutes.

■ Store the chutney in a cool, dry place. After opening, store in the fridge.

Coconut and Mint Chutney

This is a lovely, fresh-tasting accompaniment to dhals (pulses) and curries and is also great in sandwiches. It keeps well in the fridge for up to five days.

MAKES ABOUT 9 FL OZ (250 ML) Preparation and cooking time: 15 minutes	1 bunch of mint (about 7 oz or 200 g) 1 green chili, roughly chopped 3 oz (100 g) shredded coconut 2 tbsp blanched almonds, roughly chopped	5 oz (150 mL) plain yogurt 1 tsp salt 1/2 tsp garam masala

■ Remove the leaves from the mint and discard the stalks. Wash the leaves well and drain.

■ Place the mint leaves, chili, coconut and almonds in the bowl of a food processor and process until finely chopped. Stir in the remaining ingredients and mix well.

■ Chill the chutney until required.

LEMON PICKLE

There are many and varied recipes for this pickle, some using oil and spices, others using vinegar, and yet others avoiding vinegar and simply relying on the salt and the juices from the lemons. The one thing these recipes have in common is that the lemons are rarely if ever precooked. Instead, huge jars of freshly salted lemons, combined with whole red chilies, whole cloves of garlic and thick slices of ginger, are exposed to several long days of hot sunshine in the summer months to "cook" and pickle them.

Since hot sunshine is not guaranteed in all parts of the world, I have cooked the ingredients in an oven to speed up the process in this recipe. Use Indian limes if you can get them (they look like pale yellow limes), or thin-skinned lemons.

Important note: It is essential that, when preparing this pickle, your hands, all ingredients and all containers are completely dry. No water must be allowed to seep into the pickle or it will go moldy. You will need a large, clean glass or ceramic jar with a tight-fitting lid.

MAKES ABOUT 1 LB 12 OZ (800 G) Preparation and cooking time: 1 hour	1 lb 2 oz (500 g) lemons or Indian limes 12 long red chilies 3 oz (100 g) ginger 1 garlic bulb	2 tsp turmeric 3 tbsp salt 1 tsp chili powder 3 fl oz (100 mL) white vinegar or lemon juice

■ Rinse the lemons and chilies and wipe dry. Peel the ginger and slice thickly. Spread the ingredients out on a dish or a large tray and air-dry for at least 1 hour.

■ Divide the garlic bulb into cloves and peel. Preheat the oven to 325°F (170°C).

■ Quarter the lemons, slit the chilies and place in a large roasting tray. Scatter the ginger over the top.

■ Place in the oven and cook for 20 minutes. Remove, stir the ingredients, cover the tray with foil and return to the oven for another 20 minutes.

■ Meanwhile, rinse a large glass or ceramic jar and lid (needs to be a tight-fitting one) in hot, soapy water. Rinse in hot water and dry thoroughly. Please see the author's note about this on page 169.

■ Combine the turmeric, salt and chili powder in a small bowl. Gently warm the vinegar or lemon juice in a small pan.

■ Remove the tray from the oven and spoon one-third of the hot ingredients plus juices into the jar. Sprinkle on a third of the salt mixture. Repeat twice more and pour on the warmed vinegar or lemon juice.

■ Allow to cool for about 30 minutes and add the garlic.

■ Place the lid tightly on the jar and shake well to mix all the ingredients. Store for at least a week, shaking the jar daily before using.

TIP

Shake the jar every few days and place on a sunny windowsill once a week if possible to help maintain the pickle in good condition.

CRUNCHY PICKLED VEGETABLES

Another fresh-tasting accompaniment that goes well with most spicy dishes, this salad is simplicity itself to prepare. Choose any selection of crispy vegetables that are in season and full of flavor.

MAKES ABOUT 14 FL OZ (400 ML)

Preparation time: 20 minutes

3 fl oz (100 mL) cider vinegar or white vinegar
2 tsp sugar
1 tsp salt
1 tsp cracked black pepper
1/2 tsp cumin seeds

1 green chili, finely chopped
1 carrot, julienned or grated
1 bunch of radishes, thinly sliced
1 red onion, thinly sliced
1/2 cucumber, thinly sliced

■ Place the vinegar, sugar and salt into a large bowl and whisk until the sugar dissolves. Add the remaining ingredients and mix well.

■ Let the salad stand for about half an hour before serving to allow the flavors to develop.

MANGO PICKLE

If you like store-bought mango pickle, you will love the homemade one. It is packed with so much more flavor that it will make your tastebuds tingle. It is quick and easy to prepare, but requires a little patience to let it mature before it is ready to eat.

Important note: It is essential that when preparing this pickle, your hands, all ingredients and all containers are completely dry. No water must be allowed to seep into the pickle or it will go moldy. You will need a large, clean glass or ceramic jar with a tight-fitting lid.

| MAKES ABOUT 20 FL OZ (600 ML) Preparation time: 20 minutes | 6 medium or 8 small green mangoes 4 tbsp salt 2 oz (50 g) mustard powder 2 tbsp fenugreek seeds | 2 tbsp fennel seeds 2 tsp chili powder 5 fl oz (150 mL) olive oil 5 fl oz (150 mL) sesame oil |

■ Rinse the mangoes and dry thoroughly. Place on a tray or large plate and air-dry for at least 1 hour.

■ Slice the flesh along the stone, scraping off as much pulp as possible. Dice the flesh into bite-sized pieces and place in the jar (please see the author's note about this on page 169). Sprinkle on the salt, place the lid on the jar and tighten. Shake the jar well and place on a sunny windowsill for a day.

■ Remove the lid and sprinkle the spices onto the mango in the jar. Pour on the oils, replace the lid tightly and shake the jar well to ensure everything is thoroughly combined.

■ Place the jar on a sunny windowsill, if possible for at least 7 days, shaking and mixing the ingredients daily.

TIP

If you don't have a sunny windowsill, salt the diced mangoes in a large microwaveable bowl and microwave on high for 5 minutes, stirring the mangoes once halfway through. Allow to cool for 10 minutes, mix in all the remaining ingredients and transfer to a jar. Keep the jar in a warm place for several days, shaking it daily.

RAITA

Yogurt is a superb accompaniment to spicy foods and is traditionally served in some guise or another at every meal. It is a common side dish or accompaniment on the Indian restaurant menu as *raita*, lightly spiced and usually combined with shredded cucumber. Cucumber is an excellent ingredient to use in raita — it doesn't require cooking, is easy to prepare and has the right texture and mild flavor, but other vegetables or even fruits can be used to add variety.

I have used a combination of onion, cucumber and carrot but you might like to try grated daikon or radish, chopped tomato, shredded mint or finely diced melon or apple.

If you don't wish to make your own yogurt, purchase a good-quality, preferably organic, commercial product.

| SERVES 4

Preparation time:
15 minutes | 1/2 red onion, finely sliced
1 carrot, grated
1/2 cucumber, grated or julienned
1 small clove of garlic, finely chopped
1 green chili, finely chopped
11 fl oz (300 mL) yogurt (page 24) | 1/2 tsp salt (or to taste)
1/2 tsp cumin seeds
1/2 tsp garam masala
pinch of turmeric (optional) |

■ Combine all the ingredients in a large bowl and stir until well mixed. Refrigerate until required.

21. DESSERTS

THERE IS NO doubt that Indians are great lovers of spicy food. There is also no doubt that, somewhat paradoxically, a close second is their love for traditional Indian desserts or *mithai*. The consumption of mithai is more than a need to satisfy a sweet tooth; it is ingrained in Indian culture. Rich, expensive, luscious and gloriously sweet, lavishly decorated with sultana raisins, almonds, pistachios and silver leaf, mithai appears everywhere in Indian life. From birthdays to holy days, from religious ceremonies to wedding feasts, from simple gifts to lavish offerings, there is always a reason to give, receive and consume generous quantities of mithai. Indeed some occasions would simply not be complete without its presence.

Each region of India has its own specialities and there are hundreds of different variations of Indian desserts, but most are based on fresh, full-cream milk boiled down to make *khoa*, combined with ghee (clarified butter) and sugar in varying proportions. Other ingredients like besan (chickpea flour), carrots, squash, rice and nut flours are used to create different types of desserts. Cardamom, cloves, mace, and rose or *kewra* water are added to create exquisite flavors.

It was usual when I was growing up to make some of the less elaborate Indian desserts at home and there would always be a stash of *ladu*, *besan* or *barfi* to snack on with a glass of milk upon returning home from school. Later I learnt to make *rasgulla*, the most popular modern-day dessert in India, *gulab jamon*, a regular on the restaurant dessert menu, *ras malai*, and the well-known and loved Indian ice cream, *kulfi*. No party, celebration or blessing ceremony was thinkable without a selection of these essential items.

Nowadays it is rare for Indian cooks to make any of these at home, with the exception of *kheer* (Indian rice pudding), which is a simple dish to make. Superb quality Indian desserts are available everywhere Indians have settled, and, although ghee is now rarely used, the end result has not suffered significantly.

Desserts and treats

Kheer
A creamy rice and milk dessert made with basmati rice and fresh milk.

Cardamom ice cream
Homemade ice cream flavored with ground cardamom.

Mango Soufflé
A deliciously cool, light, fruity "soufflé" made with ripe mangoes and cream.

Gajrella (Carrot Halwa)
Carrots, nuts and sugar combine to make this warming, luscious dessert.

Sweet Pilau
Basmati rice cooked in saffron-flavored sugar syrup and flavored with sweet, aromatic spices.

Kulfi
A quick recipe for an old favorite, using evaporated milk, sweetened and flavored with cardamom and nuts.

KHEER

This rice "pudding" is made with basmati rice, the grains of which have more aroma and a firmer texture than pudding rice, even after long, slow cooking. I like to make this dessert with 1 percent or skim milk because I find the long, slow cooking makes the dish creamy enough, but you can use full-fat milk if you prefer, for an even creamier dessert.

Kheer is delicious served warm, or cold straight from the fridge.

SERVES 6–8	4 tbsp basmati rice
Preparation and cooking time: 2 hours	70 fl oz/4.2 US pints (2 L) fat-reduced or full-fat milk
	6 oz (175g) white granulated sugar

■ Wash the rice several times in cold water and place in a large, heavy-based saucepan with the milk.

■ Slowly bring to a boil. Turn down the heat to very low, partly cover the pan, and simmer for about 1 1/2 hours, stirring now and then. Add more milk if the mixture is too thick.

■ Stir in the sugar, and simmer for another 20 minutes.

VARIATIONS:

Stir through a couple of tablespoons of chopped almonds and pistachios, or a handful of sultana raisins about halfway through cooking.

CARDAMOM ICE CREAM

This is a really easy recipe that is deliciously creamy considering there is very little cream in it. In fact the health and weight conscious can omit the cream altogether and replace it with evaporated milk, with very little loss of texture or flavor.

If you have an ice-cream maker, you can prepare this dessert while you are eating dinner. Otherwise, it will take about 4–5 hours in the freezer.

SERVES 8–10	8 fl oz (225 mL) sweetened condensed milk
	20 fl oz (600 mL) light evaporated milk
Preparation time:	7 fl oz (200 mL) half-and-half cream or
10 minutes	heavy whipping cream
(plus churning	1 tsp cardamom seeds, crushed to a powder
or freezing time)	

- Whisk all the ingredients in a bowl. Place in your ice-cream maker and prepare the ice cream according to the manufacturer's instructions.

- If you don't have an ice-cream maker, place the mixture in the freezer. Remove from the freezer after 30 minutes and beat with a whisk or a fork until smooth. Repeat twice more and freeze until hard.

VARIATIONS:

For Pistachio Ice Cream, stir in 2 tablespoons of chopped pistachios towards the end of churning or just before freezing.

For Coconut Ice Cream, omit the cardamom, replace half the evaporated milk with coconut milk, and stir in 2 tablespoons of grated fresh coconut toward the end of churning or just before freezing.

For Coffee Ice Cream, omit the cardamom, dissolve 1 tablespoon of instant coffee in 2 tablespoons of hot water, cool and whisk in with the milk and cream.

MANGO SOUFFLÉ

A lovely, no-cook, cool treat after a spicy meal, this is a delicious and creative dessert with ripe, sweet mangoes. Pureed fruits like strawberries, raspberries or apricots could be used instead.

SERVES 6

Preparation time:
30 minutes
(about 3 hours of
setting time required)

1 tbsp powdered gelatin
2 fl oz (60 mL) cold water
1 tbsp finely granulated sugar
7 fl oz (200 mL) double cream

3 egg whites
7 fl oz (200 mL) ready-made custard
20 fl oz (600 mL) mango pulp
juice from half a lime

- Prepare six ramekins (that can hold 6 fl oz or 180 mL each) by tying a strip of parchment paper around the rim of each ramekin. The parchment paper should be positioned about 1 inch (2.5 cm) below the rim and should extend about 1 inch (2 cm) above the rim.

- Add the gelatin to the water in a small pan and soak for 10 minutes. Heat gently until dissolved. Add the finely granulated sugar and stir until dissolved. Set aside to cool.

- Beat the cream until soft peaks form. Beat the egg whites until stiff.

- Place the custard in a large bowl and stir in the mango pulp and lime juice, followed by the gelatin, cream and egg whites. Mix until combined.

- Pour the mixture into the ramekins so it comes about halfway up the parchment-paper strip. Refrigerate until set.

- Carefully remove the paper and serve with extra fruit if desired.

Gajrella (Carrot Halwa)

The combination of grated carrots, nuts, cardamoms, sugar and pure ghee produces a dessert with a lovely texture and an absolutely delicious taste. Don't compromise on the ghee though; nothing else will do for this dessert.

Gajrella will keep in the fridge for several days, but halve the quantity of ingredients if you don't want to make so much.

SERVES 8–10

Preparation and cooking time: 1 hour

2 lb 4 oz (1 kg) carrots, grated
3 oz (100 g) ghee (clarified butter, page 24)
1 tsp cardamom seeds, lightly crushed
3 oz (100 g) almonds, blanched and chopped
3 oz (100 g) pistachios, chopped

2 oz (50 g) sultana raisins
4 oz (125 g) finely granulated sugar
5 fl oz (125 mL) sweetened condensed milk
2 tbsp ground almonds

- Place the carrots in a large, heavy-based saucepan with 4 tablespoons of water and cook, stirring, on high heat for about 3 minutes. Turn down the heat, cover and cook for another 5 minutes, stirring once or twice.

- Add the ghee, turn up the heat again and stir-fry the carrots for another 5 minutes.

- Lower the heat and stir in the cardamom and nuts, saving about 2 tablespoons. Continue to cook over low-medium heat, stirring frequently, until the carrots have turned a deep orange and the ghee has started to separate from the mixture. This will take about 20 minutes.

- Stir in the raisins and sugar and stir-fry on low heat for another 5 minutes. Add the condensed milk, turn up the heat a little and stir-fry the mixture for about 3 minutes.

- Stir in the ground almonds and mix over low heat until well combined.

- Serve warm, garnished with the remaining nuts, with thick cream or ice cream. Or press into a jelly roll pan, refrigerate until firm and cut into squares. Serve with tea or coffee.

Note: This recipe works best with organic carrots as they contain less water than their nonorganic counterparts.

SWEET PILAU

A dish that celebrates the versatility of rice beautifully, this sweet, perfumed pilau is simple yet quite exquisite.

The typical beautiful deep-yellow color of this dish is unfortunately a result of artificial food coloring, but you can leave it out and have a dish that is paler in color but still tastes wonderful.

SERVES 6–8	1 tsp saffron	2 oz (60 g) ghee (clarified butter, page 24)
	2 tbsp warm water	6 cardamoms
Preparation and cooking time: 30 minutes	8 oz (220 g) basmati rice	6 cloves
	35 fl oz/2.1 US pints (1 L) hot water	2 tbsp almonds, blanched
	6 oz (175 g) granulated sugar	3 oz (100 g) sultana raisins
	1/4 tsp yellow food coloring (optional)	

■ Combine the saffron and warm water, and set aside. Wash the rice a few times and leave to drain for several minutes.

■ Meanwhile, put the hot water and sugar in a large saucepan, and place over low heat, stirring to dissolve the sugar. Once the sugar has dissolved, turn up the heat and bring to a boil. Turn off the heat and stir in the coloring if you are using it.

■ Heat the ghee in a large, heavy-based saucepan and add the rice. Stir until the grains of rice are well coated with the ghee.

■ Add the cardamoms, cloves, almonds and raisins. Stir-fry for 2 minutes.

■ Carefully (as it will spit) pour in the sugar syrup. Turn the heat down to very low, stir in the saffron water, and simmer gently for about 30 minutes, stirring now and then to ensure the rice cooks evenly.

■ Turn off the heat and let the rice stand, covered for 10 minutes. Fluff up with a fork and serve hot or cold.

KULFI

Often referred to as Indian ice cream, kulfi is still one of the most popular desserts on the Indian restaurant menu. This quick recipe cuts out a lot of time-consuming effort but still produces a wonderful result.

SERVES 6

Preparation time: 20 minutes (plus time for freezing)

11 fl oz (300 mL) light evaporated milk
4 tbsp finely granulated sugar
3 fl oz (100 mL) thick cream
1/2 oz (15 g) almonds, blanched and finely chopped

1/2 tsp ground cardamom
1/2 oz (15 g) pistachios, finely chopped
1 tbsp chopped pistachios to serve

■ Heat half the milk in a small pan, add the sugar and stir to dissolve over low heat. Cool.

■ Place all the remaining ingredients except the nuts in a large bowl, add the sweetened milk and whisk until well combined.

■ Stir in the nuts and divide the mixture among 6 kulfi molds. Freeze until completely hardened.

■ Dip the molds in hot water to loosen the frozen kulfi and serve sprinkled with more nuts if desired.

TIP

If you don't have kulfi molds, freeze the mixture in shallow pans or trays, remove from the freezer about 15 minutes before serving, and cut into squares.

INDEX